What People Are Saying About

I Drink for a Reason

"This book is a literary 'Development' from David that I found truly 'Arresting.' I 'dev'oured every word and had to take 'a rest' after reading, as I realized this book was 'ment' [sic] to be a comedy classic. This 'Arresting' comedian has 'Developed' into an amazing and insightful writer."

—Mitchell Hurwitz, producer, *The Golden Girls*

"Cross's comedy is visceral." —Associated Press

"David has composed a fascinating list of the most obscure names in Atlanta baseball history, and filled the spaces in between with some stuff. I don't always agree with him, but he always makes me think and smile, and, unlike our conversations, in this book I actually can get a word in edgewise." —Keith Olbermann

"An offbeat, pungent, and sage riot of personal essays, satire, and 'top-ten lists of top-ten lists.'" —*Penthouse*

"A few more books like this one, and we may have to get David to pull a Senator Al Franken."

—Markos Moulitsas, founder, DailyKos.com

"Immortally titled." —*Vanity Fair*

"A relentlessly funny insight into what makes David Cross honest and brutal, but above all, hilarious.   ....t."

                                                              .egg

re...

"A lightning-quick read...a great writer with a real gift for manipulating language...I could hear and enjoy his voice on every page...Fans are likely to enjoy the book."   —About.com

"...me again. I'm sorry, but there's something about David's wit and hilarious self-revelation that makes me want to jacket-blurb all over this thing. David's writing in this 'audiobook for the eyes' is every bit as funny, honest, and observant as the man himself—and, oddly, twice as smart. It's surprising and funny dot dot dot a triumph! Oh, and David, that 'dot dot dot' shouldn't be spelled out as words. It's just meant to imply I said a lot of other stuff too. Oh and obviously what I'm saying right now also isn't part of the blurb."

—Mitchell "*Arrested Development*" Hurwitz, cocreator, *The Ellen Show*

"Imagine a snarkier version of *I Hate Your Guts* (by Jim Norton), and you have REASON."   —*Raleigh News & Observer* (NC)

"Displays Cross's wicked wit, full of media and celebrity mockery with potentially offensive anti-religion commentary."

—*Salt Lake Tribune*

"David Cross is the Bruce Banner of our time, and this book is his big green monster. His energy is so intoxicating and uplifting that in some cultures his discarded bodily fluids are sold on the black market as an Irish coffee substitute. This is a great book."

—Maynard Keenan, lead singer of Tool and A Perfect Circle

"It is inappropriate for me to write a 'blurb' for Mr. David Cross, as he is rightly a legend—utterly fearless, absolutely brilliant, and a longtime inspiration to me. My endorsement would be like the weed endorsing the sun, which is to say: I live in the dirt and require David Cross (plus water) to live. But I can grow right through sidewalks, so that's something."

—John Hodgman, *Daily Show* Resident Expert
and *New York Times* bestselling author of
The Areas of My Expertise

"Hilarious, brilliant, though-provoking...Easy to read randomly while commuting to work or hiding in a bathroom stall once you get there." —*Chicago Reader*

"Flat-out hilarious...His beef with Jim Belushi is even laugh-out-loud funny." —InnocentWords.com

"Cleverly crafted." —LAist.com

"Incredibly hilarious...The quality of the humor and insights are well thought out and are written fantastically."

—*St. Cloud State University Chronicle* (MN)

"Cross's cunning use of recurring jokes and pieces written in the voice of offbeat characters seems to come from the same creative place as his sketch comedy." —*Creative Loafing*

"Cross's first book is as unique as the comedian himself, and cannot be missed." —Seattlest.com

I Drink
for a Reason

David Cross

NEW YORK  BOSTON

GRAND CENTRAL
PUBLISHING

"We Have Got to Stop Calling So Many People 'Heroes,'" "Oh, I Forgot You Could Do That," and "For the Love of God!" were previously published in *Vice* magazine and are reprinted with permission.

"Letter from the Future" originally appeared in *Playboy* magazine under the title "Dear Friends, Get Me the Fuck Out of Here" and is reprinted with permission.

"Top Ten CDs to Listen to While Listening to Other CDs" is reprinted courtesy of Pitchfork Media.

Grand Central Publishing
Hachette Book Group
237 Park Avenue
New York, NY 10017

www.HachetteBookGroup.com
Book design by Fearn Cutler de Vicq

Printed in the United States of America

Originally published in hardcover by Grand Central Publishing.

First Trade Edition: August 2010
10 9 8 7 6 5 4 3 2 1

Grand Central Publishing is a division of Hachette Book Group, Inc.
The Grand Central Publishing name and logo is a trademark of Hachette Book Group, Inc.

The Library of Congress has cataloged the hardcover edition as follows:
Cross, David
    I drink for a reason / David Cross. — 1st ed.
        p. cm.
    ISBN 978-0-446-57948-3
    1. American wit and humor. I. Title.
    PN6165.C76 2009
    814'.6—dc22
                    2009003642

ISBN 978-0-446-69771-2 (pbk.)

For me.

I couldn't have done it without you.

Contents

PREFACE   xiii

Don't Abandon Your Baby   I

But It's Good for You!   5

I Think Rich People Are Boring   9

Minutes of the Development and Programming
    Meeting for FOX Television's New Season   12

I Ain't No This or That   17

Woodstock   20

Breaking Up   23

A Non-Sponsored Look at Holidays in America   28

The Mystifying Allure of Gratuitous Luxury   34

YourStar.com   40

Scrapbooking in Michigan   43

I Would Be the Shittiest Survivor in History 48

A Little Bit about Me, 'Cause It's My Book 53

My Memoir-to-Be 62

A Free List of Quirks for Aspiring Independent
Filmmakers 65

Sitting on a Pole Trying to Win Some Money 74

Didja Know? 78

I Hate America! or, I Hate America? 80

Heaven! 85

The Five People You Meet in Limbo 89

Ideas for T-Shirts to Be Sold at Urban Outfitters 93

In Anticipation of Reading This Right Now 95

Gay Canada 99

You'll Never Guess!!! 105

Sweet Mary J. 109

Hey! Free Advice! 113

Correspondence with Dave Eggers 122

Involuntary Random Thoughts I've Had Not Always
When I Was Pooing but Certainly Sometimes When
I Was Pooing 128

Ask a Rabbi! 132

A Short Request to Lame Friends 139

Things to Do When You Are Bored 141

The Golden Age of Cowardice 145

Top Ten Top Ten Lists List 150

Bill O'Reilly Fantasy 151

Contents

How to Play "Mafia," the Funnest Yet Most Unnerving
Game Ever Invented   161

I Don't Have Children   166

A Short List of Videos with Babies in Them that
I Have Not Seen on the Internet but Most Likely
Exist and I Would Like to See at Some Point   169

Other Ways in Which Jews Can Utilize Current
Technology to Get around God's Strict
Laws for the Sabbath   171

Beef with Jim Belushi   173

Cigar Corner   178

Excerpts from the Galley Copy of James Frey's Latest
Memoir, *Lesson Learned*   183

Original Message   188

Top Ten CDs to Listen to While Listening
to Other CDs   192

An Open Letter to Larry the Cable Guy   201

We Have Got to Stop Calling So Many
People "Heroes"   210

Oh, I Forgot You Could Do That   213

For the Love of God!   217

Cigar Corner: Bonus Story!   220

Cigar Corner, Part 2   222

Truck Stop   225

Letter from the Future   229

An Afterthought   232

Acknowledgments   234

Preface

HELLO. THIS PREFACE WAS ORIGINALLY ONE HUNDRED AND NINE pages long and one hundred percent unnecessary. But a contract is a contract. Especially if it's legally binding and written in lamb's blood on parchment from olden times. I love to write. And, at the very same time, I hate to write. It's kind of a pain in the ass and really impedes my video-game playing and completion. I've written in several forms—e-mails, award-winning sketches, movies, Post-it note reminders to let the baby out, award-winning gravy-soaked possum biscuit recipes, instructions on how to use the cable remote for guests, French lessons, "The Who's #1" in drying cement—but never a book . . . until now. I like very much the idea that I'm writing a book and by extension am now a "writer," because let's be honest, no one considers sketch or stand-up "writing," even though of course it is. But writing a book, well, that puts me in the same rarified air as Voltaire or Sue Grafton or Tim La-Haye. The bitch of it all is that writing is at complete loggerheads with my desire to not be writing right now. There's a good reason I'm known for having the "softest hands in showbiz," and I am xiv

loathe to jeopardize that title. It's amazing what I will let myself be distracted by or pretend is suddenly important and urgently needs attending to, merely so that I can put off, for however brief a time, the writing that needs to be done. For example, here's a partial list of things I've thought and ways in which I have dillydallied while trying to get this goddamn fucking pain in the ass thing written:

I need to get ready for Thanksgiving.

My eyes feel funny.

I should check out some porn for inspiration.

My dog wants to play probably, I think.

Wait . . . do you hear horses?

I should really see if that wine's still good. That shit's not gonna drink itself.

Really? St. Louis is playing Pittsburgh? Huh, I should check that out. (I don't care about either team in whatever sport you first thought of.)

Maybe if I jerk off I'll be able to concentrate better. (This is then followed by an hour and a half of surfing for just the right 42-second porn clip to jerk off to.)

I swear to God I hear horses.

I should really think about doing twenty push-ups and then eventually not doing them.

Is that painting crooked?

This place is fucking dusty!

They'll be calling any second now, and rather than get started just to have to stop, I'll start writing after the call.

That call took a lot out of me. I'm wiped. Naptime!

That's not to say I don't want the riches and rewards that come with being a fancy-panted writer ("author," on the East Coast), although how this book will get written is still a mystery at this point. Perhaps an as-of-yet invented computer program called "AutoWriter" or something like that will come about. Then I can just punch in a few lines and run it through the "Pithy" program and that will be that.

I imagine that I will be asked to attend marvelous parties where witty bon mots and cutting retorts meet each other in midair where they joust in a gentlemen's game to the death. In fact I am quite sure that I will be feted at the rather large Upper West Side co-op of someone I've never met but who will host my literary "coming out" party. Her name will be something like Deidra Harwick, granddaughter of Knute Harwick and heir to the Harwick fortune. (Knute Harwick invented the non-disposable condom, look it up.) She is very generous with her time and money. Just some of the numerous charities that she works for include Operation Hang Upside-Down for Africa, Friends United to Eradicate Blind Indians, Society for the Improvement of Performance Enhanced Athletes, and Diamondcology, to name a few. I can only imagine ('cause it hasn't happened yet, silly!) what one of these soirées would be like. First there's the invitation. I suppose it's creative and artsy. Perhaps a gilded canary's head with the script written in rubies and AOL stock certificates. It is most likely hand delivered by an old Punjabi man with a sophisticated British accent. It comes at the bottom of a refreshing glass of Bombay gin over ice. "I *thought* that was a canary's head!" I will say with delight as I drain the glass and break it just inches away from the Punjabi man's head. "Of course I accept this fine, fine honor. I will see you in one fortnight. Here's a ha'penny for your troubles, good sir."

Then the big day arrives. Because I am so cool, I will ride my bike up to the imposing building, feigning ignorance that there is a town car that they've sent waiting forlornly outside my East Village apartment. "Oh, shoot. Sorry about that, I had no idea. I just rode my bike up here. No worries. It's a beautiful night out, and I rode through the park. I liked it." They will now look on me as a "real" person with no pretense or shame.

Tight, elderly women will grab me by the arm and direct me toward various groups of well-behaved and turtle-necked adults. "Look, there's Joan Von Whistler, author of *And the Devil Went to the Bathroom*. She very much wants to meet you. And in the kitchen is Donovan Yeast. He wrote that wonderful *On a Winter's Wind We'll Ride: A Susan Gerber Mystery*." I will meet them all and look down at my shoes humbly, although I will be in quiet ecstasy. I will laugh softly and secretly play with my erection through the hole in my pocket. Ha ha! That hole is from my nine-year-old pair of pants that I've kept as a reminder of when I was poor and irresponsible. Now look where they are! In a rich lady's kitchen! If my penis only knew! I will entertain . . . no, *delight* strangers with true stories of my semi-tragic youth. My broken family. What it was like to be a poor Jew in suburban Atlanta. Will there be any amongst them that can relate? Will someone step up and, through the use of a clever but not particularly apt analogy, be able to capture what it was like for me in one pithy comment? If not, I will provide the analogy myself and move on, in a feigned attempt at not wanting to make my hosts uncomfortable. "Yes, yes . . . who wants another Pimm's Cup?"

I will of course be invited to accompany my new friends on their "little vacations" to all kinds of glamorous and colorful locales. "No, I've never eaten a Plush Fruit before. I've never even heard of it," I'll say, resulting in overdramatic and urgent inhalations followed by pleadings that I must promise that I will go with them on their boat to Guigjna Island, where they have the best, THE BEST(!) Plush Fruit in the world. You can pick it right out of the basket that the local children put all their just-picked Plush Fruits in after scampering down the tree trunks. I will be sort of a mascot for these Richie Rich's—the personification of their charity and largesse.

Perhaps I will find myself in the middle of a bidding war between Grand Central Publishing and the Royal Family of Great Britain, who, after reading this book, will offer me an honorary title ship and an all-expenses paid, ten-day muckabout in England in exchange for writing a humorous calendar for them in which for each day there will appear something amusing to think about. Example: "If your sister wears the same tampon to her wedding *and* your mama's funeral . . . you might be a Redneck!" There would be an illustration to accompany the text in case of any potential cultural misunderstanding. Well, enough wasteful daydreaming. Let's write a fucking book, shall we (I)?

I Drink for a Reason

Don't Abandon Your Baby

THE OTHER DAY, I WAS DRIVING ALONG BY MYSELF IN LOS ANGELES. I was listening to NPR. An elderly woman from Macon, Georgia, was reading a story she had written for *Pecan Nights* magazine about a switch (Southern for "tree branch") she had been made to bring to a teacher to enable the teacher to punish her by beating her with it when suddenly the switch was turned to licorice by a forgiving and practical-joke-loving God. But because she was old, she was taking FOREVER to read it! Her gravelly, halting voice was barely above a whisper, and she clearly needed a drink of water. She sounded like when my mom eats bananas in silent anger. Why does NPR insist on letting its authors read their own stories? Most of them are terrible. It's painful and makes me anxious to listen to them. I slowed down as I came to a light and pulled up alongside an L.A. cop driving his L.A. cop car. Like everyone else when faced with being next to a potential bully with a Kafkaesque ability to get away with whatever they want (unless of course there's an amateur videographer nearby), I got a little self-conscious. I did what most people in cars do when they imagine cops are watching them. I fiddled with my radio like only the innocent would ever do. People guilty of crimes, no matter how severe or petty, absolutely *never* adjust the settings on their radios. This is a proven fact* and one that has guided me through many of these episodes.

As the light turned green I let him pull up ahead of me because I didn't want him to see my "I ♥ My Dog" bumper sticker on which I had Sharpied over the heart symbol and replaced it with the work *Fuck*. That bumper sticker has turned out to be one of my all-time best pickup lines, by the way. Anyway, as the cop got in front of me, I noticed one of *his* bumper stickers. Alongside the ubiquitous and highly effective "D.A.R.E to Keep Kids off Drugs" bumper sticker (remember when people used to sell and/or take drugs before that bumper sticker was conceived and applied?) there was a new, state-sanctioned, police-issued bumper sticker. At least it was new to me. It read "Don't Abandon Your Baby." Hmmm, okay. Thanks for that. I know that's not meant for me, as I am not planning on attending any proms in the near future. But has our society really come to this? I realize that our culture is so violent and we've become so coarse that we can support more than three dozen violent cop shows that feature sick killings nightly, each more shocking than the last. "Chief, we've got some sicko out there who's killing random male stockbrokers." "Jesus that's terrible." "Wait, I'm not done. And he's sawing off their arms and using them to rape college co-eds." "Son of a bitch!!" (excerpted from *CSI: Grand Rapids*.)

Do we really need to be told not to abandon our babies? Especially by authority figures with guns and shoot-to-kill dispensations? I suppose the answer is yes. It's one thing when a dear friend or family member asks us not to abandon our baby. Or even a much-loved celebrity, but the cops? Although I will concede a

---

*See: The Luzene Study, 1987.

gentleness to the pronouncement that I find interesting. Unlike the demanding and suggestively violent "Buckle Up, It's the *Law!*" one could read their own intonation into it. Say it to yourself (in your head—you don't want to end up on any lists) like an Allied confidant whispering in the ear of their lover as they stand on the banks of the Seine during the height of the student riots. Seems almost sweet. Or try saying it with a bit of wistful melancholy, like a wise old "mammy" talking from experience and passing on her sage advice to the grandchildren as they snap and de-string pole beans on the porch during a hot, swollen, summer day in Georgia. Hey! Where's that NPR lady? Maybe she could try it. She's probably just now about to finish reading her story. Just six more words to go and they can leave the station. Anyway, it takes on a different tone. It's sympathetic and well meaning. It's not at all angry. It doesn't instantly cause your rebellion gene to switch on. It doesn't make you think, "Fuck you, cop! I'll abandon whatever baby whenever the fuck I want, you fucking fascist! It doesn't even have to be a baby, either! I think I'll abandon my car, my pets, and my teeth as well!"

Which leads me to this: what *kind* of person needs to be told, or "reminded," that they shouldn't abandon their child? People who sit around all day, daydreaming and fantasizing about a future they'll never have because they sit around all day, daydreaming and fantasizing about a future they'll never have? What does it say about our selfish, stupid, and cruel society? I guess that we can be monstrously selfish, stupid, and cruel. The Iraq war (or rather the war we started in Iraq; there really wasn't much of a fight until we set up colonization school) is a good example. It's an amazingly disappointing realization to know just how thoughtless and insensitive to other human beings we can so simply and predictably be programmed to be.

Tossing a thing you don't want or no longer desire to the curb is not really that bad if it's biodegradable, which a baby is, I guess; but come on now—let's apply some standards.

Abandoned babies are unfortunate unwanted results of a once urgent desire to have an orgasm. That desire is now long, long ago in the past. A distant memory. And much like getting a bill in the mail for a nice meal you ate nine months ago, you see it (baby or bill) and think, "Huh? That was nine months ago? I'm not paying for this!!" And we toss that baby or bill into the bin. Life is cheap here in America. It's the living that is expensive. Perhaps that abandoned baby would have grown up to shoot someone point blank in the face for twelve dollars and some (admittedly) pretty cool sneakers. That's still no excuse.

Isn't that Jesus' job anyway? Shouldn't he be whispering in the fevered hallucinating imagination of the drug-addled mom while she passes by one of the hundred of thousands of churches in this country? Why is the cop forced to clutter up the back of his car with a sticker like that? That space might be better used to remind people that if a cop wants, he can beat the shit out of you and can often count on the tacit silence of a thoroughly corrupt force to get away with it. I think that might be a much more effective deterrent to would-be baby leavers. "I *will* beat the shit out of you so that you lose the sight in your left eye and pins will need to be implanted in your jaw so that you will be able to eat again if I catch you so much as even thinking about abandoning your baby!"

Now *there's* an effective bumper sticker!

But It's Good for You!

THE PREVALENCE AND SHEER AMOUNT OF "GOOD FOR YOU," "healthy" snacks is nothing short of amazing, yet completely understandable in America. Understandable simply because along with our gullibility and consumerism, we are very much fat and lazy. And we are fat because we are gluttonous. And we are lazy because we are conditioned to achieve as much pleasure as possible with as little exertion as possible. Thank you to computers for helping with that. There's no "Dear Leader" here making us eat an un-researched diet of rice and fat. No one is mistaking ice cream and candy for oatmeal and tuna fish. We just love to fool ourselves by lazily believing that massive international companies with holdings all over the world producing a hodge-podge of products like tires, C-4 plastique explosives, and paint thinner can also make "Healthy Acre's All-Natural" wholesome chocolate caramel cups—and that they really are healthy.

Have you ever been to the airport in Minneapolis/St. Paul? Or stopped in at a random Wal-Mart in wherever? They're like fat museums, half the people crawling along in those scooters.

I deeply resent the existence of those scooters, by the way. You know the ones, the "Rascal" and the "Git-Along Tubbys." And they are becoming more ubiquitous by the day. I believe their initial intent was for use by people who had circulation problems or couldn't move their lower extremities very well for whatever reason. Now people who are simply fat are using them because they're just lazy . . . because they're fat . . . because they're lazy . . . because they're fat . . . and on and on ad infinitum (because they're fat). Not to say that Americans are not wonderfully grotesque simply because an evil company tricked them into thinking they were eating pure, sugar-free manna from heaven and not the irradiated, fatty, chickenish-like nuggets filled with nitrates and ground-up chicken bones and genitalia (although the nitrates *were* heaven-sent. Fact!). No, they know what's what. It's the same thing as someone under the age of 70 suing a tobacco company for millions of dollars for not telling them that cigarettes were addictive. I have mixed feelings when I hear about that. I am (because I read) suspicious of large companies when they claim through cynical, multimillion-dollar ad campaigns designed to "nice" up their image, that they are humanity's best hope for cleaning up the mess they made in the ocean or air or ground or children. It is they and they only who are the ones who should be employed in getting impoverished communities cleaned up and lily white again. Too many people are too quick to carelessly glance at a bag of Professor McGulliver's HyperHealthy Squiggle Rinds sold in the "health food" aisle of their local supermarket and see a guilt-free snack. In fact, in a brilliant and complete understanding of their target audience, there is a line of snack food called "Guilt Free." Being "Guilt Free" can only be acquired by the practiced absence of guilt. And that's not really a good thing, when you think about it. If we didn't have guilt we'd all be figuratively fucking over our business partners while literally fucking sixteen-year-old girls in Thailand. It's not simply a matter of the physics of nature. There is certainly no shortage of wistful daydreamers of the new-age, hippie variety in America. Hell, we invented them! India jumped on *our* bandwagon! And whether it's Dr. Prometheus's Magic Agave Butter Soap Soup, or Sista Mustaffa's Hypo-Allergenic Hair Kinkifier with Nefertiti Oil, there is undoubtedly someone out there to unquestionably buy it for themselves for as long as they shall live (and/or the business isn't shut down by the FDA). And they mindlessly do this with no questions asked. Does it say "organic" on the label? Well then, by Vishnu, it's good enough for me.

With this in mind, and with a nod toward the inarguable power of placebo, I present this guideline for use by the multibillion-dollar health-food industry in order to better exploit the gullible. I'll see you on the Forbes 500 List!

Anything with "Dr." in the title is acceptable. It doesn't matter if it's food, vitamins, or sea sponges. And even if the doctor in question is a veterinarian from Greenland who got his or her license off of the Internet, it doesn't matter. What matters is that a "doctor" has given his or her seal of approval.

Make more "healthy" snacks featuring people of the clergy as mascots. Reverend Josiah Tumn's Deuteronomy 4:12 Oat Pops, or Shiek al Abu's Koran-ified Nutty Bumblers, something like that. L. Ron Hubbard's Thetan-Free Pina Colada Practical Signifiers from Planet Teegeak would all be big sellers.

Clearly, people like to feel better about themselves through a snack that is made by ex-hippies who promote meditation and astrology. And I know that it's a bummer that sometimes those snacks have to be subjected to the vindictive whims of the Imperialist Facists over at the Food and Drug Administration. But really, no one cares about how much marmoset hair there is in a bar of Jeannette's Flax Seed Spittle Bars! Let the lady sell her wares!

I would encourage someone to market the following snacks based on the ghosts of heroes past: Harriet Tubman's "Now That's What I Call Freedom" Twisters, Doc Severinsen's Beauty Flakes,

Jimmy Cliff's High Times Protein Photo-Shopped Cookies, Jim Valvano's Pumpkin and/or Coconut Golden Bricks, Anne Boleyn's Pussy Juice Bars. Ewww, really? Forget that last one.

Also, one last thing, if someone could get back to me on it: I believe that there is a cream you can buy that is owned by the Dutch that has been marked down to around eight dollars. This cream, when rubbed liberally on your target area, will "melt the pounds off." Why isn't this cream more popular? People should know about this cream!! Tell people about this cream, goddammit!

I Think Rich People Are Boring

With an apology and all due respect to Louis C. K., who has done a bit using this premise, I think rich people are boring (too). And by that I mean unimaginative. I'm sure they are at least somewhat interesting. Telling tales of throwing up in different countries with diplomatic immunity and hiring the Rolling Stones to play their daughter's christening and then giving Mick an extra hundred to let them blow him in the bathroom while he hums "Start Me Up." But besides the obvious, what do they do with all their money? Sure, they buy things, and companies, and people's lives to assure their continued wealth for generations to come, but outside of that, what? I mean, if you've literally got *billions* of dollars and you buy an island, several mansions, yachts, and planes and shoes and lobster dinners and you still find yourself with 800 million left over, take at least *some* of it and have some fun! I saw footage from Jack Welch's wife's birthday where everyone was upset at the lavishness. I was way way more upset at how lame it was, given that he spent a gazzibillionish dollars on it. "Living statues?" Come on, that's bullshit. You've got billions and billions of dollars! Get creative! How about choosing one species to make extinct. Just randomly pick one and buy them all and then kill them. You get to play God. That's one thing that I might do.

"I don't want any more Nicklebacked Stingface frogs."

"Daddy, what ever happened to the Nicklebacked Stingface frog?"

"David Cross bought them all and killed them." Wow!!

I would buy the rights to a word, maybe the word *maybe*. And every time you used it you would have to pay me. And you would have to pay me in kisses. Or every time you used it you would have to say "David Cross's maybe." As in, "Hey, if we get there early enough, David Cross's maybe we can get tickets." Or, "Fuck you! Did you ever stop to think that David Cross's maybe, just David Cross's maybe that I love you? David Cross's maybe you're right."

I would have a HUGE fireworks display, I mean the biggest, grandest one ever. It would be an annual event and it would last for, like, almost twenty-four hours. It would fill the sky and be able to be seen for miles. And I'd have it on July 3 on the Canadian side of the border.

I would have bionic shit installed in me exactly like the Six Million Dollar Man. Actually, I take that back. It should be a lot more than that. I mean, what's six million dollars to me? That's like twenty-five bucks to you. So no, let's make it 60 million dollars of bionic shit. *The Six Million Dollar Man* was on thirty years ago, back when six million meant something; now a third of all children under ten in America have six million dollars. "Hey kid, where'd you get that six million dollars?" "Oh this? The Tooth Fairy." My bionics would get me super hearing and super seeing (but just in one eye), super touching, and the ability to do upper, genius-level yoga without an instructor present.

I would have surgery so that I would literally fart a hundred dollars, so I could say to the condescending jeweler who I was trying to buy diamonds to have surgically implanted in my extra heart, in a very snotty, cavalier way, "Do I have enough money?! Dude, I *fart* hundred-dollar bills" and then prove it. People would be repulsed, but then they'd secretly be psyched also. You would be in an elevator and let one rip and everyone would be like, "That is disgust . . . oh . . . look at that." And you could give them the hundred-dollar bill and say, "Sorry, here."

You could re-create Hell. Like Neverland Ranch or when you're traveling down South and there's a huge themed place some crazy town character has spent his life and fortune on. Like the Flintstones thing in South Dakota. And it can really be like Hell, too: It would be a thousand degrees (or whatever temp it says in the Bible), and there would be a huge, muscley, really cut Devil with a huge cock like in Japanime. And you could have tortured souls in a lake of fire, but since you couldn't use people because it really is hot, you use animals dressed as people. Dress an antelope as Hitler and dolphins as SS men.

And there would be very thick, fireproof glass so that you could tour and look through it. And you could have different rooms that held different real people based on the ideology of the tour group that was attending. Are they right wing? Hey, there's Abbie Hoffman, and Larry Flynt, and Madalyn Murray O'Hare! Are they left wing? Look, it's Margaret Thatcher, and James Dobson, and Karl Rove!

I would buy a radio station in the middle of nowhere—some country/soft hits station outside of Cheyenne—and then hold a contest to win a truck or something. But the contest would be who can sit on top of a pole five hundred feet in the air for the longest without giving up or falling off. And the second place prize would be a year's supply of Sindex, the "x-rated window cleaner." Then I would just hire a helicopter and drop shit on them like hams and eggs and I would let some other rich friend of mine hover over them and take a dump! Ha!!! Don't worry, I'll pay for the charges.

Minutes of the Development and Programming Meeting for FOX Television's New Season

Meeting was attended by: Tina Wrash, Head of Programming; Dallas Treasure, Head of Marketing; Janet Woo, Head of Talent Relations; Cindy Fleer, Head of Comedy Development; Peter Branson, Head of Drama; Thurman Stye, Head of Dramadies; Lisa Quinn, Head of Reality Development and Implementation; and Dr. Owen Stillhog, Head of Publicity. On speakerphone from his blimp hovering just above the building was Rupert Murdoch, Owner of Most Everything. All were accompanied by various assistants who will be known simply by a number.

8:02 Nova lox on the deli tray discovered by Tina to be "oily."

8:03 Lox thrown out of window into parking lot B. Meeting adjourned until new "less oily" lox can be secured.

8:23 Meeting reconvenes. It was discovered that Rupert Murdoch had been on the phone the whole time. He wakes up and continues his money breakfast. Tina's Assistant #3 reads from the Overnights. *America's Nudest Teens* wins its time slot, retaining 86% of its lead-in, *Monkey Rip!,* and has the biggest share of the most coveted demographic, the 15-to-65-year-old-age group. Lisa Quinn buzzes for one of her assistants to run in and pat her back.

8:28 There is some concern that the Friday night lineup is susceptible to the latest CBS offering, *CSI M.D., Law Town,* the latest number one hybrid show. Lisa suggests FOX should counter with a show that has been in the pipes for a while now, a reality game show called *Muslim Hunt.* The show is being developed with the cooperation of the new Public Broadcasting System and everyone (mysteriously, she pauses to wink here) is really behind it. Dallas says that he has some great ideas for this one. He suggests that there could be a tie-in with *American Idol* or any of the franchise's spin-offs, mentioning *Algerian Idol* several times and bringing up his desire to get "our hooks" into the New Iraq with *Iraqi Idol.* He notes that the number one show in Iraq is *Blow Out.* Tina interrupts Dallas to take a call from Assistant #3, who is seated three chairs away to her left. The assistant informs Tina that her meeting with Doug VanEllin, her lifestyle consultant, about a new iPod playlist that he has designed for her has been pushed back to noon.

8:32 Dr. Stillhog brings up a problem he is having with some of the cast of *Donovan's Wharf.* He has tried unsuccessfully to get both the teenage lead actors, Devlin Reece and Strawberry Williams, to participate in an online charity event to raise awareness for a fake disease, which is currently being configured based on polling the show's demographic. Dr. Stillhog is asked what his course of action has been. He says that he promised them the covers of *Paper* magazine, appearances on the *Tonight Show,* as well as "bumping up" the gift bag with more secret swag from the FOX Swag Vaults in Yuca Valley. The reason they are hesitant to participate is that both of them get "grossed out" by diseased people. Tina asks what kind of punitive measures have been threatened, to which Dr. Stillhog replied that he had threatened a ban on scented candles or small dogs in the trailers. There was general silence until Rupert spoke up.

"It's Rupert. Just like the voice of God, hmmm?" Everyone laughed at this for over nine minutes.

8:41 After the fake laughing died down, Rupert spoke up again. "These two kids, Devlin and Strawberry . . . kill them, chop up their bodies, feed them to the rest of the cast." Tina argued that when that tack was taken with Hunter Rain from *So, You Think You're So Smart* it backfired and there was a crew mutiny. "Bumblefucks!" said Rupert. "That was a reality show about NY waiters being switched with retarded summer camp kids! This is different!" "I was going to say that, too, Mr. Murdoch," Lisa Quinn said. The issue was decided that they would base a reality show on which actor to kill and eat.

8:47 Lisa Quinn pitches a new show. She said that she wanted to pitch a show based on the current success of Martha Stewart's ability to convince people to look up to her although she had gotten caught and convicted of a crime in which she was, in part, lying to the feds. The show would be a reality show featuring a recently convicted celebrity wherein cameras would follow every moment of the trial and jail time. "Who's the celebrity?" was asked by several people. Lisa Quinn: "Ummm, how about Megyn Nero? She's the lady from CourtTV who got caught shoplifting upskirt videos from a store in Van Nuys."

Rupert again: "Bloody bushberries! Let's do one better. Let's frame a celebrity with a crime, and then we'll be there from the very beginning! America will go apeshit for that!" Everyone was enthusiastic about this, and after debating various celebrities and crimes it was decided that Katie Couric would be framed for selling nuclear secrets to China as well as child endangerment and kidnapping, which would be accomplished by burying alive her son Vaughn in a 6' x 6' pit in the back of her house. "Git-r-Done!" Rupert said, imitating his favorite comedian.

At 9:02 Assistant #2 (me) received a call that Andy Richter was downstairs and very upset, arguing with a security guard. It seemed that someone had thrown a bunch of lox all over the seat of his opened convertible. Everyone laughed and Tina opened the window and yelled down to Andy: "Hey Richter, did you see the overnights for your show?" She then started throwing all the food out the window onto Andy's car. Andy started to half laugh. Then Rupert told the driver of his blimp to position it over Andy's car. As it did, the bottom hatch opened up and Rupert's bare ass was soon poking out. As Rupert started relieving himself (and you could hear the grunting over the speakerphone) he said, "Thank you." And left.

The following shows were discussed and are now being produced for FOX's Reality Channel:

America's Least Favorite Horse!

Infant Swap!
> Two infants from two different families are swapped for the first five years of life.

Line Wait!

I Can Make It Cheaper!
> Contractors bid on public housing contracts.

So, You Think You Can Projectile Vomit!

Now That's What I Call A.I.D.S.!

America's Next Top Bottom (for the Logo Channel)

What Time Is It?

Judge Baby
   A three-year-old makes decisions in small claims court
   based on its dysentery.

Are You Smarter than an Elderly Retarded Chicken?
   Delighted contestants from Oklahoma play tic-tac-toe with
   an elderly retarded chicken and sometimes win.

Last Blogger Standing

You Asked for It!
   Lawyers from one of America's top law firms are covered
   in caramel and honey and airdropped into the Amazon
   rainforest.

Making the Cut A reality show about mohels.

What the Hell?!
   Ben Stiller stars as the unfortunately but comically named
   Lenny Shittingsly, the neurotic but likable put-upon
   schnook who gets stuck with the unfortunate task of trans-
   porting his wife's dog, who can't stop farting, to the MTV
   Movie Awards (played by Will Smith), in this adaptation of
   the popular comic book character.

Who Wants to Marry My Midget?
   It follows *Exploiting Gullible Teens* and *How Low Will
   We Go?* on Tuesday nights.

I Ain't No This or That

It's been noted by literally hundreds if not thousands of folks that I am contemptuous and patronizing. I think part of the reason for that is because I am an athiest, and inherent in that belief system is "I think that I am right and therefore, since you believe the opposite, that you are wrong." And inherent in *that* idea, hidden underneath layers of generational begrudging but still civil respect, is the idea that people who have the benefit of freedom of choice, and still believe in their respective religion, are foolish. Or rather, it is a foolish thing to believe in, given the holes in logic and scientific refutation and plain, old honest facts and practical theories that go a long way toward postulating how the Red Sea could have been parted or how one day's worth of oil could have been miscalculated and actually could reasonably last for eight days without God's hand or how Mohammed would not have frozen his nuts off while ascending to heaven on his magical winged horse; etc.; etc.

Okay, fine: I'm contemptuous and patronizing. But I'm not simply some knee-jerk lefty with a soft spot for a more equitable distribution of wealth and state-sponsored health care. (Not exactly correct except for the state-sponsored health-care part. Just simply as a practical matter of fiscal responsibility. I don't want no A.I.D.S. babies bringing me down!) For instance, I am not opposed to the death penalty for certain crimes. In fact, not only am I not opposed to it, but I heartily condone it for certain specific situations. I have heard many compelling arguments against it, but I have not been swayed. I'm talking strictly about the idea of state-sponsored death as a moral issue. Hey, look, I don't want the governor of Mississippi* deciding on the fate of my life during an election year any more than you would, but I think if you fuck a child to death, you should die. Done deal. No debates about your shitty upbringing or drug-induced devil state, please, I'm late for dinner.

The guilty don't have to die in any horrific way. It can be peaceful. This isn't about something as intangible, and ultimately unsatisfying, as "revenge." Just . . . that's it. You take a life, you give up your right to live. Why can't that be agreed upon by everyone? Even lefty hippies. That seems fair. That's one of those little things on the plus side of being an athiest, no conflicting rules within your prescribed religion in which you have to pick, and then justify, a side. As I mentioned earlier, I know that there are often very good arguments against capital punishment. The most undeniable being the mountains of innocents put to death based on the rash judgments of the ignorant who are ruled by their emotions, or worse, the corrupt. But seriously, you kill two elderly people for some crack money, you die. I don't care if you sober up and realize you've done a naughty thing.

---

*Also, who is the governor of Mississippi? Is there an actual governor of that state? There must be. Total redneck, right? I figured. How proud is he of his state being at the bottom of virtually every major "quality of life" category? I bet there are people in war-ravaged Chechnya who would get to Mississippi and feel like even they had gotten stuck in a backward time warp.

I also believe immigration is a legitimate issue and that handing out fliers to remind everyone that immigrants built this country doesn't matter. While it's true, and a nice thing to remember, it is of zero relevance today. I believe that the Koran is a violent tome whose teachings go against everything this country stands for and people who subscribe to it are suspect. We've already got enough crazy lunatic religious zealots in this country, so let's not add so many of their sworn enemies that I have to live in fear of the coming crusades pouring down Fifth Avenue just when there's the big annual sale at Barney's.

Let's see. What else can I tell you to put a wedge between me and annoying lefties? Oh, how about this?

Woodstock

I AM WELL ON RECORD STATING MY DISDAIN AND CONTEMPT FOR hippies (idrinkforareason.com/austinhippieriff). Any new-age, gytronics-Pilated Stevie Nicks wannabe armed with enough Dr. Bronner's soap and a bushel of sage can, and will, tell you in five "Oh wow, man's" or less what's wrong with the world/America. But they will consistently be erroneous because they will have left themselves out of the equation, and they are very much a part of what's wrong in America.

But how can they be part of what's wrong with America? They leave most of us alone and don't impose their illogic on others. Yes? They are a simple and passive breed of drum-circling do-gooders. Right? Right?! Mmm, not really. Just as they might correctly consider all outdoor advertising (billboards, advertecture, etc.) to be eye-rape (or whatever half-assed cutesy name they might call that), I consider all of their riot of colors and stupid bumper stickers to be eye-rape as well. And the kind of eye-rape that leaves you with an advanced case of eye-AIDS to boot.

I've always hated bumper stickers as a way to communicate.

They're fine if you want to show your support for the Steelers or trumpet your child's academic prowess. It's the bumper stickers that espouse ideology or a political point that I can't stand. There's a smugness and cool detachment to them that I don't care for. As well, they are usually completely ineffective. As far as I know, neither Tibet or Mumia or Leonard Peltier is free. Kids still use drugs, war still wages across the world, and we still proudly trade our children's blood for oil.

I would like to force them to "Practice the Random Acts of Kindness" they feel are so important on unsuspecting and uninterested fellow passengers and see what those people think. Will they change their attitude once they see that no one really wants to learn the zither or know how to make a compress out of cow dung and boysenberries to help get rid of crow's-feet? There are numerous epicenters of this kind of community across America, and I've been to many of them. But there is one that stands a bit taller and sillier than the rest. No, not Boulder or Taos or Marin or Eugene or Burlington. It's Woodstock, NY. There is a shop there—let's call it "The Lavender Buffoon"*—that features a pet psychic. A pet psychic, you say? "But that's ridiculous. Just being a psychic is ridiculous already." Yes, they've taken perhaps the oldest and scammiest of the scams and kicked it up a level. And there are enough deluded idiots up there to financially support it.

There are few greater proponents of absolute, improvable hucksterism than psychics. And I am including anyone involved in religion. The ability to convince intellectually weak suckers that not only can I tell you what tidings or warnings your long-dead uncle wishes to impart, but I can also tell you if your fish is feeling melancholy, or if your black Lab, "Howard Zinn's People's

---

*Not really. The lawyer said I can't say the real name (but trust me, it's way better than the one I just made up), although you might be able to find a picture of the shop placed somewhere else in this book.

History of the United States," really wants to go back and visit the apartment you used to have in the city. Just for this alone we should do something about these useless people. Maybe tax them more. Create a "well-meaning, but actually harmful" tax so that when they advocate drinking and bathing in your own urine, they also pay into a universal health-care system to offset the damage brought on by drinking and bathing in one's own urine.

How am I supposed to take you people seriously? Which, ironically, is the single most important thing to you. You so desperately want to be taken seriously, not dismissed with a lethargic wave of the hand, but to have your ideas considered and one day in the future implemented (for that's when your utterly unrealistic, juvenile, *Marxism for Dummies* utopia will come true). You really believe in Magick? Really? You believe that burning or ingesting the right combination and exact measurements of fungus and herbs will draw a lover forth? I will give a pass to my friends and loved ones who believe (sorta) in Jesus and/or God and all of that nonsense because they've been brainwashed since birth. But Magick?! That's something you have to, as an adult, think about, consider the real possibilities of, and ultimately accept. As a thinking, rational, educated grown-up. There's no brainwashing involved. Half of this planet doesn't and hasn't celebrated "Magick Day" for the last two thousand years. There's no universal culture surrounding it. You were never taught that if you didn't believe in Magick that you would burn in hell for all of "eternity." No, you're just desperate for something to attach yourself to that will give you some form of (to you, at least) unique identity. Never mind that if you move to a place where everyone thinks like yourself you've pretty much drained the "unique" factor from it. Oh hippies, when will you ever learn?

I would like to preface this next piece by stating that this was originally written over three years ago when the following was new, raw, and pertinent. Since I experienced all of this though, I am happy to say that I have met the real *love of my life (seriously, for reals this time) and am happier than I could ever or have ever imagined. She's a combination of Glinda the Good Witch; Dorothy Parker; a young, alive Natalie Wood; and Sacagawea at her hottest all rolled into one perfect woman. Also I* never *posted this anywhere. I just wrote it for me. And now, you.*

Breaking Up

MAN, AM I SHITTY AT BREAKING UP WITH SOMEONE. BOTH THE doing and receiving. I mean we all know that there are some people out there who are basically impervious to this kind of pain. (And I speak in the present tense, because the—what I thought was—love of my life just broke up with me and moved out of our apartment six days ago. It all happened rather quickly. I mean, of course she had been wrestling with it for a while, but I didn't have the benefit of being privy to all of her private thoughts. It's only now I wish that she had had a diary that I could've found and lost her trust by reading and finding out how she felt. A real diary, I mean, not some online attempt at making yourself matter to strangers through unsolicited opinions and slander.) What was I saying? Oh yes, how do they do it? The ones that either cause the pain or have their lives irrevocably altered yet are out at Jigglers three days later doing chocolate cake shots with that girl who works in the shipping department and then fucking her, while unknown to both of them, her five-year-old kid silently watches from the hallway? It takes me a month at least to be able to even get it up after something like this. Maybe I need to read more men's magazines ("fish in the ocean" and "This is Denise, who says that the best guy to go out with is a guy on the rebound, 'cause they're the easiest to manipulate"), but I'm usually a big pile of near catatonic whimpering for at least the first week. Actually, I should amend that. I always seem to have an almost admirable stoic and serene acceptance of the inevitable as well as a truly honest attempt to reach out and help the very person that is not just breaking my heart but adding another layer of solid injury, distrust, and cynicism to the rock-hard crystalline sheath that forever protects my once innocent, healthy heart.

I want to be him . . . or her, either way. Just not me, I guess. Oh. There's another bad part of getting dumped. (Which somehow doesn't seem an appropriate word for three and a half years with relatively no problems and cohabitation. *Dumped* seems like it should only apply to relationships lasting a year or less. After that the word should be something like *killed* or *temporarily deaded*.) Suddenly the ubiquitous empty greeting of "Hey, how's it going? How are you?" becomes the most loaded question since "Are you now or have you ever been a communist?" The simple answer is never very simply put. "Oh, I've been better." "Why, what's wrong?" "Well, my girlfriend left me and . . ." Cut to three minutes later, and your friends are shifting uncomfortably trying to get away while you talk about how you just bought her a $400 coat and asking "What's the matter with me?"

And you want to call but you can't (the inner dialogue is the worst) because you will be perceived as annoying. So then you think, "Well, that's unfair to her. I shouldn't keep calling even though that's the only thing that makes me temporarily feel better." Why am I being so fucking nice and cool about this? I should be sending dead rats with torn pictures of us in its dead rat asshole. No, no. As satisfying as that would be, I'll look like the biggest asshole on the planet, and everyone except for people like Neil Strauss will lose what little sympathy they had for me. Neil Strauss, of course, would consider me a hero.

I become a mess of a human being, both physically and spiritually. I don't sleep for three days, then I sleep for a week. I can't read, I don't eat, and I have to take psylium husk just so I can take a shit that *doesn't* look like a Fallujahan checkpoint. But then, one day, about two weeks in, mysteriously (but not really, because it happens like clockwork every time), I bounce back. Brighter and better than ever! Suddenly I am filled with the energy of a JV squad on their first trip to Hooters. I become a mix of Steve McQueen and Hank Williams Jr., and I will literally fuck anything that moves and is also a girl. Haha! Now I'm in the revenge phase! The predictable and temporary two weeks where I'm going to improve myself and make her jealous. I am going to be the ultimate perfect guy filled with secret talents that you'll never get to the bottom of in this lifetime. I'm gonna learn French. And I'm gonna go to cooking school. I'm going to become a certified daredevil, too. Maybe I'll go to one of those pussy-eating classes that extremely ugly feminists featured on HBO's *Real Sex* 23 run out of their Topanga Canyon house. That'll show her.

Next time I see her and she asks how I'm doing, I can say, "Pretty good. C'est plu pas ne (etc.). Oh, that means I'm doing well, thank you. Hmmm? Oh, it's French. I totally speak French now. It's too bad you left me or I'd make you some double-cut lamb shank with a béchamel sauce and Madeira reduction with a side of . . ." Ahhh, it doesn't matter. Nothing you do will matter.

You could work out, get six-pack abs, get all your teeth fixed and whitened, be nominated for a humanitarian award for your work in the Congo with Doctors Without Borders, show off your bullet-hole scar that you received whilst working for them, and win the lottery on your one day off, but no. It's over. So now you deal with the pathetic knowledge that nothing will be the same as it was an hour ago. You will both be varying kinds of weird around each other forever. Forever. Forever ever. Now the unspoken as well as the ill-timed and urgent things unfortunately spoken aloud will float around just above your head. It's like a gauze veil that you can see through but still blurs your vision.

There is the forced and hyper "Hey, I'm over it!" phase that, even if you know it's coming, still has the ability to kick you in the ass. It starts with the brain trying to trick the heart and ends with your heart getting *super*-pissed that the brain even dared to bring it and then kicks your ass twice as hard as it did the first time. You convince yourself that you're okay, even though you have been sharpening your sitting-and-staring-at-inanimate-objects skills to the point where you can peel paint with your mind!!

And guess what? You'll do it more than once, too. Maybe a half dozen times. "Hey! I'm totally over it! Awesome!" You call your friends and they're truly excited that finally you're your old self again and you wanna hang and you make plans to meet up and go to Lit, and then the next thing you know, you're in the grocery store staring at the apples and crying.

Time out! The following just happened for real: I just ran into my ex on the street in front of my building. (Let me point out quickly that in a remarkable show of consideration and under-standing of what I may be going through, she thoughtfully moved a mere six blocks away.) As fate would have it I ran into her while hungover and carrying a load of dry cleaning. We had some more tremendously awkward chitchat about nothing (I am about as im-portant as an issue of *Us Weekly* to her) and then had yet another in what will be a never-ending series of awkward exits. "Well, I guess I should get going. This stuff isn't gonna dry-clean itself!"

"Oh, brother," I muttered to myself as I turned away. Sometimes you just feel like Charlie Brown but a real one, not a two-dimensional black-and-white line drawing. Such is the totality of the rejection of everything that is "you." It's all part of it, though. The natural healing process that seems to take forever while experiencing but is summed up by a dismissive "Yeah, that was a fucked-up time for me" once it's finally over and done with.

Here is something that should help you, although it never works nearly as much as it should: First and foremost is the knowledge that everyone (and I mean everyone, even Hugh Hefner) goes through this. Your personal hell of betrayal and recrimination has been shared by everyone from Onan to Mohammad to Helen Keller and Sienna Miller. You are not alone, but of course, you are. You could get one hundred freshly dumped people in a room and after just a couple minutes of commiserating they would retreat into their overactive imaginations and fester there.

All the happy, colorful misremembered but authentic images of the two of you. The happy couple from a month ago . . . all lies. The over-romanticized stained-glass tableaus of you and her (or him) from the first time you met, kissed, shared Valentine's Day, told each other you loved them. There you are! The innocent pie-eyed lamb being circled, considered, and sized up for the slaughter by a cunning wolf. A soulless, evil, heartless Nazi monster cunt of a wolf.

Which brings me to Valentine's Day.

A Non-Sponsored Look at Holidays in America

VALENTINE'S DAY

I'VE BEEN ON EVERY END OF VALENTINE'S DAY—IN LOVE, IN UNRE-quited love, in hate, happily solo, depressingly solo, and drunk, high and wired with my dick hanging out in a closet at some strange coke den in Chelsea. And collecting the cumulative experiences into one well-rounded observation, I conclude that Valentine's Day seems to be a bit cruel if not entirely unnecessary. Not the idea itself but the idea put into practice. When you add up the numbers, the odds are very, very good that *most* people will feel some degree of shitty on February 14. And knowing that Valentine's Day means hundreds of millions of dollars for the greeting card, florist, restaurant, condom, porn, and eating-an-entire-bag-of-Dorito's-in-one-sitting industries doesn't make it feel any less shitty. Valentine's Day is only enjoyable if you're in a solid, good relationship, which applies to how many of us? Twenty-five percent, maybe? Maybe. For everyone else, it sucks (idrink forareason.com/valentines). It's a constant reminder (starting with whatever lead time the aforementioned businesses decide is needed for a "killer V-Day," blowing the previous sales record out of the water. High five, Stevens! Your idea to make chocolate-covered roses with butter-toffee-flavored condoms for thorns—brilliant!) of how miserable you are even though two weeks ago you didn't seem really all that miserable or preoccupied. You didn't really think about it that much. But now! Loser!!! At best, Valentine's Day is a nice opportunity to take time out of your tiring and unadventurous schedule to appreciate your partner. So what if it's obligatory? You still get a nice meal, get to re-member what you love about each other, and fuck. Unfortunately for the most of us, there is a much greater chance of it being an awkward night teetering on the cusp of derailment with merely the twitter of a butterfly's fart. Perhaps you have just had a huge fight over something trivial that got blown way out of propor-tion and turned into something else altogether?* Are you on your third date, so you don't know how much gravity to assign this Valentine's Day date? Ignore it? Bring her a card? Bring a card and flowers? What? Thinking of breaking up? Just received your mail-order bride who doesn't understand your crazy American custom and won't leave the train station? Were you just caught masturbating by your partner? Just discover you have breast can-cer? I could go on and on.

And here's the ultimate aggravation: not one of the happy couples around actually need Valentine's Day either. It's always

---

*Examples:

Why don't you like the color purple?

Someone's a pillow hog.

I don't want to fucking watch *The Wizard of Oz* again!

. . . well then, YOU fucking drive!!

I don't care what it's supposed to be made of; it made me sick!

How can you spend that much money on baseball cards?!

I didn't know there wouldn't be any hot water left! It's not a fucking conspiracy!

You used to fuck a magician?!

You really, honestly believe that the Spin Doctors were underrated?

Valentine's Day for them. It'd be like having a nationally recognized Celebrate Your Perfect Health Day. We'd all have to spend the day watching a bunch of content, fit people flaunting themselves in front of the rest of us. People with limps, coughs, acne, glasses, crutches, and/or wheelchairs. That's what every smiling, laughing, squeezing, kissing couple is on Valentine's Day. Unwittingly adding a teaspoon of bitter stomach acid to be drizzled over your heart like so much Malbec reduction sauce over your prix fixe duck confit. Everyone knows this, too. It's not like it's some mystery. It seems that the only people who really benefit from this day of forced love are those Casanova con artists from Italy or France who come to America and take a bunch of frumpy housewives and widows for all their worth, or frumpy housewives in long-ago loveless marriages who subsist on reduced-fat cookies and delusion. Oh, and the makers of Stetson cologne for men and lastminuteflowersforfuckups.com. My point is that it's more hurtful than helpful.

Although I suppose it is nice to celebrate. And there's no better way to celebrate something than fucking. And there's no better way to celebrate the fact that you're fucking than coming. So, all in all, I guess it's better than Flag Day.

PRESIDENTS' DAY

Wha . . . ? Are you serious? Go fuck yourself. Presidents' Day. Please.

HALLOWEEN

Halloween is probably my least favorite of holidays. The reason is twofold: one, because it points out in a personified way just how sexually repressed we are as a culture, and two, because it points out in a physical way just how uncreative and easily amused we are as a culture. As for the first part, come on, we've all seen the idea of "sexy"* applied to a number of Halloween costumes that border on the disconcerting. It's one thing for Pam in Accounts Receivable to get liquored up and wear a "sexy" (for the remainder of this piece, please imagine all uses of the word *sexy* to be in quotation marks— I don't want to keep doing that as it will soon turn distracting) cat outfit or nurse outfit or cheerleader ensemble or whatever classic (Harem concubine!) sexy Halloween outfit has become the safe "go-to" outfit for the masses. But these usually have the opposite effect on me (not that anyone's wearing them with "catching me" in mind). I find myself more turned on by the girl who dresses as a sexy hobo. That's weird! And who wouldn't want to fuck a hobo? How about a sexy pigeon costume? Or an erotic AIDS patient?

The other thing I, on a more specific and personal level, don't like about Halloween is that it's got a real "amateur hour" vibe to it for me. Excusing the irony, I wouldn't get on a soapbox and lecture about this, but I just feel like I do this sort of thing all the time because of my line of work. So donning a wig and beard and period outfit is no big deal. I can't share in your giddy enthusiasm about your Gandalf thingy. I imagine it must be similar to how alcoholics feel on New Year's. "Amateur hour," they think as they pass out in their puke. "I do this almost every day." Or maybe it's similar to how the rich treat Christmas—with a sense of the distinctiveness surrounding the day, but really, it's not that special. "What? Taking a vacation and opening up presents? I do that virtually every day. I'm not trying to be a dick, but . . . I'm rich. Think about it." Or maybe a better example is how the mentally ill must feel on Ash Wednesday. "Yeah, yeah, yeah, you put strange markings on your face because an invisible man told you to." Surely

---

*This being subjective, of course. For some seeing a woman in pigtails wearing skintight footie pajamas with the ass cut out and clutching a teddy bear is disturbing; for others it's highly erotically charged. No judgments, it just is.

someone *must* spend Ash Wednesday thinking to themselves, "I feel like a fucking idiot." What is this, the fucking Dark Ages?

THANKSGIVING

There's a bit of cognitive dissonance involved with this holiday as you get older. You are celebrating sustenance and family and a vague attachment to the founding of this country, which seems to lose its glory with each bit of information about how we really got this land that sneaks its way through the fairy-tale police. Thanksgiving is not an easy day to celebrate because of this. On the one hand you have the simple, universally relatable theme of taking one day out of your busy, increasingly impersonal life to appreciate and be thankful for what you have* and on the other you have the shameful actions of a bunch of elitist racists who thought nothing of killing savages in preemptive actions because they weren't "civilized" (and they had all the corn). And we all know how that worked for the people who lived here already. If they weren't being killed and having their land stolen from them, they were being tricked into keeping warm under a blanket knowingly infested with smallpox that a generous federal agent donated to them. Of course, years later they got us back by rigging their slot machines to play extra tight, but what are you gonna do? At least they can get a family of five hammered on half a case of Milwaukee's Best, and that's nothing to drunkenly sneeze at and then wipe the snot

---

*Except for people with diseases and life-altering debt. It's funny how so many great, and not so great, literary stories or movies adapt the similar theme of how a poor family with seemingly nothing can be happier or more at peace or laugh more than a rich, well-fed family who have grown detached because they bicker over their money or for whatever reason. *A Christmas Carol,* or *It's a Wonderful Life,* or *Fieval—An American Tale.* It's all a childishly optimistic view of reality. It's what lets us ultimately mitigate the slaughter in [fill in the name of country where poor people are being rounded up and killed]. "Those poor, terrified, malnourished people probably know a greater joy from just being alive and sharing a piece of week-old nan around a dung fire than I do, especially with all the shit I'm getting from McCready in Development. Christ, I wish that asshole would get off my back!"

on the sleeve of your filthy Wisconsin Badgers sweatshirt you got from Goodwill. That's a *huge* savings over the years! But I do enjoy the story about them teaching us how to make popcorn. Obviously this was before we slaughtered them. I wonder if that was the first time popcorn was eaten in a "snacky" way. By the white man and his family as they watched the slaughter. Also, what's up with oyster stuffing? Makes no sense on paper.

MY BIRTHDAY

While I realize that this is not yet recognized as a federal holiday, by the time this is published, if my agent is worth his commission, it will be. What will I have done to earn this? Uh . . . does the gift of laughter mean anything to you people? How about developing little-watched TV shows? What about my work with the folks at the Office Depot over on Broadway and Eighth? How about teaching indigenous tribes in the Amazon rain forest how to dig for fresh water and creating viable aqueducts?* My birthday should be a day of celebration and somber reflection, rather than what it is now—a day of mourning or penance.

---

*Soon.

The Mystifying Allure of Gratuitous Luxury

idrinkforareason.com/luxury

As I continue my toddle through this life that others have chosen for me (I'm talking to you, God! What was the deal with the Red Sox blowing that 5-run lead to fucking Kansas City last Tuesday? And how about that crazy thing with You getting me drunk and then having me accidentally run over that boy's dog, killing it? What were You thinking?), I will on occasion have a momentary lapse in my endless habitual daydreaming where I will see things in a clear and stark way that point out some absurd human foible that, although a ubiquitous part of my life, I hadn't really noticed before. That's my gift. And it's a shitty gift too, so don't get jealous. Some people refer to this as an "epiphany," but I think that might be a little too grand. It suggests an angel's knowing hand in the whole thing.

The latest in these tiny "What the fucks?" occurred early yesterday evening as I was in my hotel room pooing. I was experiencing a particularly bad spell of IBS that saw me cramped and on the toilet with my arms uselessly wrapped around my stomach as I leaned forward in some involuntary sense-memory reenactment.

I had left the bathroom door open. (Why wouldn't I? It's my room, and also there was a full-length mirror on the inside of the bathroom door, whose existence has always bothered me, as I don't like to watch myself taking a shit. Maybe if I was German, but I'm not. I'm one hundred percent American, so suck it, Lou Dobbs!) Anyway, while I was sitting there the maid knocked on the door and announced, "Housekeeping." I panicked, but because I was all cramped up, all I could manage at that moment was a weakly croaked, "No!" She clearly didn't hear and knocked again, saying, "Housekeeping, turndown?" I said, louder and much more urgently, "No thanks, I'm in bathroom!" Except she did that thing most hotel staff do where they will open the door as they're knocking and announcing themselves. I yelled, "I'm taking a shit!" as she turned, looked, and, having no choice in the matter, smelled. She was as embarrassed as I was (Perhaps more so: I think hotel maids are often like black bears—they're more scared of you than you are of them, and all they really want to do is just root through your trash), and she quickly backed out, averting her eyes, apologizing the entire time, and that was that. Now, that alone didn't bother me. In fact I found it pretty funny almost immediately, as well as being a top candidate for a good story to relate to my friends and family at the upcoming Thanksgiving Throwdown my sister sponsors. What does ever so slightly bother me, though, is the reason she was going to enter my room in the first place. She was there to administer the "turndown service." She was given a key to my room for the sole purpose of turning down one of the corners of my bedsheet and to leave a small piece of chocolate on the pillow. Thank you, but no. The sight of a mini chocolate on my newly exposed pillow does nothing for me. Absolutely nothing at all. Am I to be filled with the warm, comforting sense of being cared for by a nurturing Dominican grandma? The wholly satisfied feeling of being luxuriously pampered by an unseen but benign corporate nanny? I find it odd that this practice exists. The idea that after a

long, tiring day in a strange town or even stranger culture, that I've
come "home" to a place where a strange lady of decidedly lesser
economic class and status is dispatched to my room to move my
sheets around and leave a tidbit of chocolate like some lazy, under-
achieving elf.

Similar to this is the men's room (or ladies' room) attendant.
Unlike valet parking—which, while not completely necessary, actually serves a useful (while arguably gratuitous) function—the
men's room attendant is useless, save for people with advanced
arthritis or unbendable elbows. The feeling of easy, cheap elitism
is inescapable. There's a nagging sense of, "Hey, you might be having a bad day but at least you're not stuck listening to and smelling
the greasy, vodka-soaked explosive shit splatters of people enjoying yet another night out." It'd be one thing if the attendant was
a twenty-five-year-old frat guy named Joey standing around in a
mesh Giants jersey, but it's always a black guy or Mexican, and
about eighty percent of the time he's about sixty and moves with
sadness.

There are numerous examples of what seem to be wholly unnecessary and ultimately laughably ineffective attempts at luxury
foisted upon the unwilling in this way. When I travel first class on
planes, I don't like being addressed by my first name. I don't like
being addressed at all really, but I suppose there needs to be some
way to get my attention to find out whether it's going to be the
balsamic vinegar or creamy peppercorn dressing. I don't like being
approached, and I watch as the stewardess squats down in front of
me, puts her hand on my knee, and, as she displays the DVD selec-
tion, asks me, "David, will you be joining us at the movies today?"
This really happened, by the way. But I'm getting off point. This
is about excess.

I have a friend who is a bit Jappy. And by that I mean that she is
a Jew who is whiney and deeply concerned with her own comfort
at all times. What did you think I meant? That she is cute and shy

with horizontal eyelids, looks great in a private school uniform, and is a bit subservient? No. Anyway, the other day this friend told me (this is all true, by the way) about how she has been getting massages once a week at her house. She pays a licensed massaging man to come over with the full massage kit (table, scented oil, candle, and ironically ineffective "atmospheric" CD featuring the sound of cicadas, running water, and plinkety New Age electronic harp and soft techno whistles and farts) wherein he plies his trade. She's mentioned this a couple of times and I've never really commented on it past a "That's nice," or "That sounds great, maybe I should do that." That is, until, after mentioning it again, she added the following stunner: "I usually get a four-hour session." Huh? Four hours!!??!? Who the fuck gets a four-hour massage? People with severe physical disabilities maybe, and even they're probably thinking, "Okay, enough's enough" around hour two and a half. Four-hour massages are exactly why people hate Hollywood. Come on! That's got to be one of the more indulgent things I've ever heard of. Have you ever received a *one*-hour massage? As nice and relaxing as it is, by the last ten minutes or so, you get so antsy for it to end so that you can check your messages or at least just get out of the "virtual, New Age woods" you're lost in. Of all the examples of indulgence that the idle rich might indulge in, this would have to be right up there at the top of the makes-very-little-if-no-sense-list to hardworking people whose idea of a holiday is waking up, walking ten feet to the porch, and drinking themselves into a stupor while they daydream about all the unimaginative things they'd do if they won the lottery. ("I'd quit my job and move to the Haunted Mansion at Disney World! Just make them build me an apartment there!" or "I'd get super fucked up and buy a bunch of cars and just shoot them!") There's a surprisingly large and extensive industry that caters to the super-duper rich.

I saw on one of those "magazine" shows, *Dateline* or something, a titillating story about high-end luxury items, and I swear to you that I am not making this up. And I grant that a lot of the examples I use to illustrate a point I'm trying to make are logical but fabricated extensions of what I find absurd, but this is not one of them—this is true, I swear it. One of the items they showed was a 24-karat gold inlay for the sole of your foot that fits inside your shoe. What the motherfucking "f"?! Jesus, why not just have diamonds surgically implanted in your heart? Gold does serve a handful of useful purposes—it conducts electricity, doesn't tarnish, is very easy to work with, it alloys with many other metals, it's widely used in the aerospace and medical communities—but what purpose could it possibly be used for as an instep? You don't even get to show it off, so there's no real gratification in even that. I suppose you could take your shoe off at dinner and say, "I know you have to go up and accept your Pulitzer in a minute, but check this out!" As I am writing this I realize that there is the equivalent of the golden instep for every economic class out there. This next item isn't exactly gratuitous luxury, but I would put this in the subset category of unnecessary items. I've seen this around a couple of times now. It's called "the bumper badger," and it's a thin, corrugated piece of rubber that latches on to the inside of the trunk of your car. It hangs over the back of the exterior and protects the bumper—the bumper of your car, of course, being the thing that protects your car. The bumper is usually reinforced rubber or plastic and is designed to take the impact of a hit. So this thin piece of nothing is there to protect the bumper from scratches, I guess? So in order to keep the back of your car looking pretty you have to drape a goofy piece of rubber mat over it? Kinda defeats the purpose. So many things that are presented to us as "time savers" or just regular "thank God somebody finally figured out a better way!" type of items are wholly superfluous and not really needed.

You can see it in the perpetually empty smile of the models performing mundane, everyday tasks in the ads throughout the Sharper Image or Sky Mall catalogs or in any given infomercial.

Folding an easier to fold ladder, storing something under your bed with ease that up until now was not possible to store under your bed without fifteen seconds of focused imagination. The joy of finally cleaning your gutter without having to stand on something to elevate you. Making pancakes without all the muss and fuss that you used to endure with the new "30 Second Pancake Batter Thing!" How did the pioneers ever do without it!? Jesus, we are a lazy, gullible, mindlessly consumptive culture, aren't we?

YourStar.com

I don't get it. Well, I get it in the sense that I understand what it is. And I get why, given the intelligence and gullibility of Americans, it not only exists but also truly thrives as a business. But, come on, paying money to a suspiciously generic-sounding company called the Universal Star Council to have a star named after you or a loved one?! You're kidding, right? You're not? Go to www.yourstar.com, you say, and I'll see what you're talking about? Okay, fine! I will!

The home page of yourstar.com features the promise "As your star shines . . . your love will last. Eternal beauty, and infinite possibility mingle among the stars, and now, one of them can be yours . . . 30 day guarantee—imagine the look on their face when you give them their very own star, officially recorded with the International Star Council!" (At least it did before I started making fun of this.)

Okay, I'll do just that. All right, give me a minute here to let me stop laughing. Hang on. Man, this is taking longer than I thought. Okay, here we go. Nope, still laughing. Need another second here.

I snotted myself a little. Let me wipe. All right, I'm done. Let's see now, hmmmm, I'm imagining a look comprised of a mixture of incredulous outrage and pity. Is that right? A look that says, "How motherfucking dumb are you?" You named a star after me? Which one? Point it out. Oh it's "up there somewhere"? Wait, you can narrow it down to the Crab Nebula? Well, that'll save some time in finding it. What the fuck is wrong with you? I'd rather have a gift certificate to Shit Farm Indian Food Diarrhea Outletters. I'd rather have forty dollars' worth of henna tattoos on my face. What does that even mean, you named a star? Why not just name a microbe after me? Or anything else equally intangible and impossible to see after me? What happened, they ran out of cubic inches of Atlantic Ocean to name for me? How about a "patch of air" over the Rhine? What about the Queen of England's next fart? Can I get that named after me as well? Why stop there? What about truly imaginary things that, for a nominal fee, can be named after me? I'd like to name the next sighting of the Loch Ness Monster after me, for $39.95. How about the whisper of an angel? For an extra fifty bucks I'll throw in its celestial "aura" up to, but not exceeding, a radius of six inches. And seriously, the "International Star Council"? Again, you're joking, right? What do you have to do to be a part of that "Council," provide proof of citizenship from a country on Earth, while being able to look up and point? What kind of scam is this?!

I'll tell you what kind. The sweetest of them all—the perfect kind. Is this for people who don't believe in angels (because "believing in angels is ridiculous") but do believe in the power of transcendental meditation to create an energy shield that would turn back nuclear missiles? Because that makes complete sense. First of all, who's going to dig around to find out who to check with about whether there's really a star named for you, and then actually check? No one, that's who. And if anybody does check, all you have to do is show them some bullshit certificate-looking thing that you can print off of your computer at home with a heretofore unknown font declaring that your star name is sanctioned by the "ISC"? They actually have a thirty-day guarantee. In case you get a sudden case of the "What the Fucks"? or "your star" red dwarfs and explodes in the next few weeks.

I'm imagining something like that. Am I close?

Scrapbooking in Michigan

RIGHT THIS VERY SECOND I AM SITTING IN THE BAR AT THE Sheraton in Novi, Michigan, just outside of what used to be Detroit. The name of the bar is 21.1.11, which is the zip code for Novi, except broken up by periods. The bar is very much your typical corporate hotel bar. It is just off the lobby and visible to everyone from every angle. There are two flat-screen TVs showing various football or baseball games. In between the games they show FOX News. I've been a regular here for the last two months while I shoot a movie here in Michigan. Like pretty much every hotel, the drinks are outrageously overpriced. But I get them back by never paying any money for the coffee that's set out in the morning at their "honor bar."

There have been many groups that have come in and out of the hotel for a day or two or three while I've been living here. Nothing too exciting. A wedding occasionally will liven the place up, but mostly it's groups of people belonging to the Michigan Psychoanalytical Foundation, or a company of regional tire salesmen, or Peggy Hartford's 85th birthday party or some such thing.

But today is different. Today promises a wealth of emotions and involuntary judgments. Today there is a scrapbooking convention taking place. The name of the company holding the convention is Close to My Heart, and they use the word *convention* in a literal sense. It's less of a celebration of great scrapbookers or a sneak peek at some of the new items in the scrapbooking world that will soon be entering the market, but more of a get-together of women who would normally be doing this at home by themselves or with a couple of friends. But here, for an all-inclusive fee, they scrapbook with hundreds of like-minded strangers. All women. Not even older gay gentlemen who dress like Mr. Rogers and whistle Lerner and Lowe tunes while wearing half-glasses. Not even one! There's nothing really on sale here. No new scrapbooking technology being shown off, just the scrapbooking itself. There are a couple of seminars throughout the day, but outside of that it's pretty much just the act of scrapbooking. That is to say, pasting photos on pages and then decorating the edges around the photos with various seasonal or occasionally appropriate stickers and cutouts. Is it a photo of last Halloween? Then add a pumpkin! Are you memorializing Brittany's baby shower? Then add a cartoon of a stork and a pacifier!

Scrapbooking seems to me one of those things that you don't really need any help with. It seems like something I could figure out on my own without having to spend ten hours in a seminar. I'm a heterosexual male, but still.

I met two of the several hundred women in town for it here at the bar just last night. They were very excited to take a picture with me even though they weren't exactly sure of who I was. They were, however, confident that I was on TV or in the movies or both, so the picture was requested. I commented on what I saw as maybe being unnecessary—the need for "instruction" in scrapbooking—but they assured me that it was all part of the process. Now I am going to have to stop for a bit because they are

coming out of the ballroom where they were "cropping" (which
is when everyone scrapbooks amongst each other in a fun way to
bond after a long day of seminars). I mean they are pouring out in
droves and are now starting to swarm the bar in the way that only
large groups of middle-aged scrapbookers from Ottawa on one of
the few "vacations" they'll go on this year can. I better go upstairs
lest anyone see what I'm writing and get upset. Okay, I just read
this over and I want to say that it was rude of me to put quotes
around the word "vacation" back there. Just because they're not
scaling Machu Picchu or exploring the Cenotes of Mexico or having their senses ramped up to 1,000 at a Russian disco in Ankara,
Turkey, as the very large man who literally pulled you in from off
of the street now grips your thigh under the table so hard it's bruis-
ing while promising you that the women who are trudging about
unsuccessfully pretending that they aren't high and/or sex slaves
are clean and love Americans* doesn't mean that they haven't in
the past or won't in the future. These scrapbooking women *are* on
a vacation, even if only in the sense that they are away from their
families or solitary, unexciting lives back in Grainy Lakes, Ohio.

There is more than a little irony to the fact that this very event
is something that one would imagine would merit being "scrap-
booked." That the time being spent here by these women (and one
gay man—I was wrong), hunkered down over an officially sanctioned "scrapbooking scrapbook," remembering better times that,
obviously, weren't spent at the Sheraton Novi, remembering other
memories. I walked down to the Grand Ballroom where they are all
meeting and I am going to take a rough guess that there were about
350 women seated at the long tables that had been put into rows
stretching from one end of the hall to the other. Were it not for the
faux gold leaf on the walls and fake crystal chandeliers, you might
think you had stumbled onto some room in China or Mexico or

*True—I've been there. I'll save it for the memoir.

the Mariana Islands where the local ladies were assembling vibra-
tors for a penny a day. And in what could be viewed as either irony
or unremarkable happenstance, depending on your view of all this,
"Almost Paradise" from *Footloose* was playing at full volume as the
ladies unwound from the day-long seminars (including one called
"Crop Talk"—no kidding) by applying their newfound pasting
skills to photos of them drinking margaritas at newly single Tonya's
apartment, where they all watched the *Project Runway* finale.

I was looking in through the open double doors from what I
thought was a safe distance, in the hallway with my back against
the far wall, but the two ladies from last night saw me within seconds. We talked briefly and they filled me in on what was going on.
That's how I now know the term *cropping*. It's fun to have terms
and abbreviations and just generally make up your own language
for your hobby. It lends a sense of exclusivity and insider standing.
Earlier that day I had walked through the parking lot of the hotel
so I could go across the street to Best Buy and get a video game (my
own stupid but fun time waster) and walked past at least a dozen
cars with some form of "Close to My Heart" adornment on them
as well as the Christian fish symbol thing that some Christians
put on their cars to let other drivers know that they don't believe
in most science. This does not in any way surprise me. In fact it
goes a long way toward validating my cocky, assured judgments.
The kind that piss people off when you see a bunch of overweight
women in sweats and U of M (or W or O or I) T-shirts, reeking of
drugstore perfume, lugging crate after crate of scrapbooking para-
phernalia and a case of Mountain Dew through the hotel lobby,
greeting everyone by name in an accent that would make the characters in *Fargo* seem like students of Henry Higgins, while a bag of
Doritos and a six-pack of Seagram's Peach Fuzzy Navel stick out of
their homemade Kid Rock purse, and you say out loud, "I bet half
of them have those little Christian fish things on their cars. Wanna
bet? Anyone?"

Hold the phone! It is now October 3, I'm still at the Sheraton, and the entire second floor and a couple of banquet rooms on the first floor are being taken over by *another* scrapbooking outfit! This one is called "Creative Memories." These ladies make the "Close to My Heart" women look like lazy pieces of shit that just crawled out of an iron lung so they could go take a nap on the couch. These women are scrapbooking on steroids and acid times ten meets the Wolfman!! As I said, they've booked the entire second floor and are having scrapbooking sessions that start at eight in the morning and go to eleven at night! Jesus. What? I don't understand.

I've met a number of these women in the past few days, and they all seem genuinely nice, but this is starting to feel sad. I went walking up and down the second floor with its walls the color of blisters and its cheaper-by-the-ton, not-so-stain-resistant carpeting, peering into rooms with titles like "The Charlevoix" and "Isle Royal" that seem more like prison rec centers and less like "banquet" rooms. Barely anyone talking, all hunched over their scrapbooks, lifting their heads occasionally to nibble on snacks. It's easy to project "concentration" into robotic movements, but this is utter boredom at its utterest. And this is, I suppose, a slice of the "real America" that so many Republican candidates have been prattling on about. Here in Novi is where the values of small towns triumph over their big-city brethren through sheer moral force, reducing everyone in their path to a quaking shell of a supposed human, boo-hooing apologies, bent in contrition, while the weight of all their elitist wrongs renders them in mute awe of the righteous. Well, I've seen enough. I wish these women well, not only on their current projects but also in the sufficient attainment of future memories. At least as much as necessary to bring them back to the Sheraton Novi/Detroit next month.

Go Lions!!!

I Would Be the Shittiest Survivor in History

I WOULD BE THE SHITTIEST SURVIVOR IN HISTORY, I DO BELIEVE.
Not that this is something I'm proud of—more like an ambiva-
lent realization I came to while in line at Whole Foods. I was buying twenty dollars' worth of olives—that is to say four ounces
of olives, but it's worth the exorbitant cost to lessen my carbon
footprint. (I'm concerned what people six thousand years from
now may think of me.) Anyway, lately, for no specific reason,
really, just pure coincidence, I've been watching a lot of docu-
mentaries and Discovery Channel and History Channel shows
that have a "survivor" theme or are simply "tales of harrowing
survival." Whether it's one person stranded by themselves seriously injured in a forest buried under a mountain of fire ants or a
small group of people who run out of gas in an arid, unforgiving
desert or a large group who get stuck in a surprise killer storm
on an icy mountaintop, I've witnessed dozens of reenactments
and even actual footage that the survivors had the wherewithal
to document. Brutal, torturous, forever life-altering struggles to
live. And I'm not talking about that silly TV *Survivor* reality

nonsense where the winner gets a million dollars for basically going without chocolate for a month and shitting in a hole in the ground. I'm talking about people who, less then "cheating death," survived on a courage most of us will never know—a staggering primal fortitude that is often said to be inherent within us all but, for me at least, is highly doubtful. I'm talking about when a plane crashes and there's one survivor, lost at sea, freezing cold, holding on to a floating chunk of foam core trying not to think about sharks too much but rather concentrating on figuring out the best way to drink their own urine (much harder to do if you're a girl).

Man, that is *not* for me. I would be working on a way to drink so much seawater that I would get all filled up and drift off to a nice post-meal nap that I would pray I would never wake up from. Did you read about that teenage girl who was kidnapped by a well-armed stranger and taken cross-country against her will and managed to leave clues to her whereabouts and outwit her kidnappers leading to her rescue? Those are the tales of survival I'm awed by. Now, I like to think I'm somewhat clever. Certainly if you were to see the terrarium I made in sixth grade for Ms. Kowalski's science class (currently on display at the Carter Center in Atlanta) you'd give me the benefit of the doubt. But I think if I found myself in any of those situations I would likely end up a pile of cowardly bones somewhere, providing an unexpected yet delicious carrion treat for the locals. Have you seen *Touching the Void*? Have you seen or read about Shackleton's *Endurance*? Or better, how about the guy who had to s-l-o-w-l-y chop his arm off at the elbow with a pocketknife because when he was rock climbing his arm got stuck and he couldn't get it free and he knew that no one was gonna be coming for weeks and he knew that it was the only way he was going to have a chance at getting down and remain alive? Are you kidding? I'm such a pussy, I'd still be dangling there today, a funny-looking skeleton with glasses.

There's no way I could go through all that shit. I'm not sure it's even about the pain. I think that the nagging feeling I have even in the best of times (pizza party!!), the feeling that I don't think life's all that great, would take over eventually. I don't have kids, so I won't go through the "I've got to do it for the little ones" phase that might imbue me with superhuman strength. Perhaps in Day 2 of my dilemma, hungrier and weaker in mind and body, I might think about my baseball cards I want to get back to, or the new Radiohead CD due out next week that I was really looking forward to, but will that really keep me going? Nope.

I don't even know the first thing about survival. There are at least a dozen of those bathroom books with subtitles like "Everything you ever wanted to know about how to get out of every situation ever—and ten you don't!" that tell you to punch a shark in the nose or to tell a bear it's stupid and things like that, but come on—punch a shark in the nose? I guess I'd do it, but I would have already started the flashback of my life well before I balled up my fist and put on my best shark-punching face—i.e., I would already have given up and started saying my goodbyes. If I were lost in the desert by myself, I would just lie there and cry for two days and then spend the rest of my time alive trying to use my shoes to light a fire or something equally as inane. I would probably go through a brief phase of hitting rock bottom and then having the epiphany and accompanying surge in strength where I would stop feeling sorry for myself, rising up and yelling out to the stars, "Get yourself together, dammit! You've got to do something or you're dead! Now think, motherfucker!" before I got tired and looked around for a relatively comfortable place to lie down and die. As for kidnapping, well, I'm pretty sure that if I was kidnapped by brutal forces, dragged around, and beaten regularly but then found myself with a risky but maybe my only chance to try and escape, I'd probably still be hanging out with the kidnappers asking them if they wanted tea and did they need me to drive.

Now on the other hand, if I was on one of those *Survivor* or *Survivor*-lite reality shows, I think I would do quite well. If I knew that the sound crew who were just out of frame could ultimately save me or set a broken bone or give me that fucking chocolate bar that every privileged egotistical crybaby with no true sense of sacrifice seems to miss in a way so histrionic it would make Al Pacino multiplied by Nicolas Cage divided by Tyra Banks blush, I would be able to get through most any "survival" condition in which I found myself (in the month we were shooting). Now that I think of it, though, I suppose that if I were in a real, honest-to-goodness true survival situation, I would at some point become aware of the financial and sexual rewards awaiting me if I were to survive my ordeal. A book, film rights (and since I am an actor, potential work playing the older version of myself in a fictionalized future scene. The younger me would of course be played by Orlando Bloom or Jude Law, whichever one is, as of the publishing deadline of this book, "hotter" in accordance with the scientists at *People* magazine). A separate book about the making of the film and how harsh the conditions were would be in the offering, too. It would be called *My Story's Story*, and it would explain in detail how the cast and crew had to make due with very few modern amenities. (No Kiehl's Green Tea Infused Eyelid Lotion available, or those towels that I like from that nice hotel in Milan, and also that time when we ran out of Mandy Patinkin's* favorite pita chips etc.) Then a documentary film of the book about how difficult it was to make the movie. *My Story's Story—The Real Story Behind the Story.* Kind of like *Heart of Darkness* or *Burden of Dreams* but not a straight documentary. More like *Touching the Void* but without the real danger of death and the awe-inspiring triumph over it through superhuman strength and courage. I could then write and produce

---

*Mandy would play my mom.

a one-man show off and then on, and then off again, Broadway about my experiences of turning the graphic novella written about the financing of *My Story's Story's Behind-the-Scenes of the Making of The Story Casino,* which was thematically designed and inspired from the story the way I told it on a special sixteen-part *Oprah.* My point is this: I would be filthy rich. But ultimately, what we learned here is that Mandy Patinkin not only loves pita chips but that he has a favorite kind. Can you guess what they are? Answer at the end of this piece.

Oh! Hello! It's the end of the piece!

Answer: Roasted garlic!

A Little Bit about Me, 'Cause It's My Book

"I'VE BEEN TO PHOENIX, ARIZONA, ALL THE WAY TO TACOMA, Philadelphia, Atlanta, L.A. Northern California where the girls are warm so I could be with my sweet baby, yeah." Steve Miller sang those words and, thanks to the borderline tragic need of aging boomers to remind themselves of a fantastic youth that is more than likely 75 percent imagined, probably still does at the Verizon/Delta/Capri Sun amphitheater near you. By the time I was in my early twenties I had been to all of those places (yes, even Tacoma), living in two of them for at least nine years and another for six months. I'm using this to illustrate the point that, because of an unstable childhood in which my family moved at least once a year if not more, and because of an early entry into the world of stand-up, traveling "the road," I too, like Mr. Miller, have been all over America. The only states I have not been to are Alaska and North Dakota, and North Dakota doesn't even count. And Alaska is so far away that it might as well be Tasmania. And to say you haven't really been to all of Australia just because you didn't go to Tasmania is silly. So, I've been all over America.

People are often lulled into attributing blanket generalizations to people of different regions—i.e., the good folks of New England are tight-assed and prudent, people in the South are friendly and move at a slower pace, people in the Midwest are useless tweakers who don't shower for weeks on end, etc., etc. Sometimes, of course, there are some truths to these assessments. People in the South are, indeed, on the whole, more "polite" (in the sense that they say "hello" and stuff like that) than most other masses of people. That's not to say there aren't any racist assholes who would shoot a hippie faggot in the back rather than hear about two of them getting married in a strange progressive land far, far away. And I'm sure there's at least one person in the Midwest who's not selling her nine-year-old's pussy for another hit on the ol' glass dick. For the most part, these generalizations exist for a reason. I am going to do my best (through my thoroughly jaded jaundiced eyes of biased bitterness) to convey what a day or lifetime spent in some of these charming hamlets of carefree nuclear families grilling their bulk-bought Mexican hot dogs and scooping potato salad from a five-gallon plastic bucket, is like.

Let's start with where I was born and where I return to at least a couple of times a year—Atlanta, Georgia. Now I don't want to turn this into a memoir, as I'm a bit young for that yet. But I do have some pretty amazing stories to tell. You can turn to page 62 for a teaser of some of the stories I'll be relating in the memoir that will be forthcoming at some point down the line. When people find out that I grew up in Atlanta, they will usually say, "Where's your accent?" which is ridiculous, since everyone should know by now that I sold it to Larry the Cable Guy for twenty bucks and a set of "Git-R-Done" tire covers. Actually I grew up in Roswell, a sleepy (read: boring) suburb just north of the city. Now it's all connected and pretty much part of the poorly planned sprawl of Greater Atlanta (see "The City in Mind" by James Kunstler for a sensible, well-researched essay on how and why Atlanta blew it), but back when I was a kid it wasn't.

Not everyone acquires an accent from wherever they are from. How come Jewel doesn't sound "Alaskan"? Why doesn't Stephen Colbert have a thick South Carolina drawl like that retard who works at the "Lil' Peach" on Sundays? What about Amy Sedaris? Or David Sedaris? Or Dan Rather? He's from Texas, for chrissakes! What about James Taylor? He's from Martha's Vineyard. Why doesn't he sound like some elitist, liberal Kennedy-lite asshole? And how about Marlon Brando and Johnny Carson? They were from Nebraska. How come they didn't sound like horses? Etc., etc. But as I've said before on my Grammy-losing* CD *Shut Up, You Fucking Baby* the Southern accent, in particular the "redneck" accent, the accent of the stupid and lazy, is mysteriously the most ubiquitous regional accent in all of America. Outside of the annoying upspeak of teenage (and not so teenage, sometimes) girls—which is its own, albeit less mysterious, phenomenon—the redneck accent can be found in places as diverse as Modesto, California; Hot Springs, Arkansas; and Cumberland, Maine. I don't know why. I'm no sociologist, so stop asking. It just is.

One of the more curious but lasting things about the South is the amount of science/blacks/Jews/fag/progessive-liberal/secular atheist/foreigner haters that particular region has a history of producing (albeit thankfully decreasing) and the corresponding cultural vacuum that exists outside of the larger cities. Is there a correlation to be made? Probably, but that would just open me up to cries of "elitist" or "condescending prick." Hey, come to think about it, that doesn't sound so bad to me. Who's gonna call me a condescending prick, anyway? Jeanette Dunwoody? That Baptist

---

*I lost to Weird Al Yankovic, but so did Garrison Keiller, who might be the only human less funny than Whoopie Goldberg. What am I saying, that's absurd. Whoopie Goldberg hasn't said one goddamn funny or original thing in her life.

homeschooling mom who will never even read one of my dirty devil words, or Cooter Dupree, that government-cheese-eating, welfare-soaking asshole alchoholic who does nothing all day but watch *The A-Team* and mildly torture his dog? I don't give a shit about them, anyway. Nope, most likely I'll be set upon by the other kind of narrow-minded, tone-deaf clown that is the biological sister to the lunacy of the well-heeled, Jello-salad-serving pride of the South—her counterpart to the northwest.

The northern Californian über PC, well-meaning but sadly feckless lover of all living colors of the rainbow, be they black, white, brown, yellow, blah blah blah. I loves me a good hippie/ "anarchy now" dialogue. While there is very little if nothing I can appreciate about the couple in Vernon, Georgia, who will stamp their feet in anger and twist and sputter about at the idea of two gay guys in San Francisco who want the right to be legally recognized as married, I do somewhat empathize with that same gay guy who is upset with my "intolerance." But sometimes it gets out of hand. A couple of years ago I did a show in San Francisco. I usually have pretty good shows there, but quite often, and this has been true of doing shows there my entire career, I will face pockets of invariable and wholly predictable PC anger at something I've said. By far, most of the time the audience has my back, and if they didn't necessarily agree with my point, at least understood the exaggerated comic intent of the bit. But sometimes sincerely well-intentioned people are so overly sensitive and myopic that any sense of irony, parody, or satire is squeezed out of the bit, leaving a bone-dry statement devoid of humor lying dead on the hot sidewalk in its wake.

At this show I did a bit that at its core was about how an atheist running for office in America (this was in 2006 during the beginning of the primaries), no matter how viable, equitable, and universally accepted his ideas for improving the lives of all might be, will never be a major party candidate in my lifetime. Then I talked about how Mitt Romney (who was doing very well at the time) could very likely end up being the Republican nominee and then talked about what he, as a Mormon, believes. Obviously there are no jokes in the above. I just wanted to give you a synopsis of the bit, which was probably ten minutes long and wouldn't translate all that well on the page. So I did the bit, made my point, and moved on to some hilarious abortion jokes. A couple of days later, because back then I was foolish and vain enough to have a "Google Alert" for myself, I stumbled upon a blog entry from someone named Emily who had been at the show. Here it is, quoted in its entirety from the blog *SFist:*

SFist was excited to hit SketchFest's Comedy Death-Ray act last night at Cobb's. The lineup (full of *Mr. Show* and *I LOVE the '80's alums*) looked promising. After the usher told us to give him $10 we landed front-row seats. Which served us well for the surprise star of the night, Paul F. Tompkins—who had by far the strongest set of the night. Seriously, give that guy his own TV show! The other notable act was the vocal stylings of Hard 'n' Phirm, who ended the night with their rendition of a Latin power love ballad, which brought down the house, and which *SFist* is secretly hoping someone will sing to us this Valentine's Day.

SFist, like most of the crowd, were there to see David Cross, and able openers only served to increase our anticipation for his set. Cross's work on *Mr. Show* and *Arrested Development* are some of the funniest in contemporary comedy. Sadly, *SFist* was really disappointed (*appalled* might be the better word) by David Cross's routine. In addition to getting the smallest laughs from the crowd, it was the most blatant public display of bigotry we've witnessed in person.

It's difficult to define the difference between making fun of something and attacking it. It's a fine line, but many comics get it right: the greatest cultural and religious satire takes the beliefs held by a group of people and spins it to show the comedy inherent in those beliefs. For example, *South Park* has covered the very same ground in terms of joking about Mormons by going through the Joseph Smith story (which was what Cross went through as well). *South Park* explicates the story to hilarious (and irreverent) effect by making it into a musical, complete with ditties about translating golden plates, angels appearing, and the plates conveniently disappearing whenever outside sources ask for evidence. Cross, on the other hand, simply laid out the story of the religion's foundation, and at the end of major points essentially said, "Isn't that dumb?" "Can you believe how stupid these Mormons are?" Baddum-chee! Get the joke? We didn't. Showing why something is ridiculous is comedy, telling you it's dumb is more of a soapbox lecture. People at the club paid for comedy, not a lesson in religious beliefs punctuated with statements like "How dumb is that?" The letdown here is that *SFist*, like a lot of fans there, were hoping for the type of awkward comedy Cross does best, not the kind of bit you'd expect from a talk radio show host.

It was surprising and a little confusing that a comedian of Cross's stature and talent would spend so much time on pure vitriol. Cross seemed to deflate some of the exuberance of the evening (which was buoyed by a strictly enforced two-drink minimum), and the lag showed with paltry applause. Moreover, his bit seemed derivative of recent attacks on Mitt Romney's candidacy that have appeared in *Slate* and elsewhere, and which are based not on his political record so much as on his Mormonism (which is the way Cross began his piece). The difference is that the *Slate* authors weren't trying to be funny. Any religion, plus political aspirations on the part of one of its adherents, could equal pure comedic gold, given a proper witty treatment. Sadly, Cross fell short of the task he set himself. Cross ended his piece with "Mormons are F***ing idiots"—not one of the more socially tolerant statements we've ever heard. But hey, maybe nobody told him it was Martin Luther King Day.

I promptly wrote back, which I rarely do because as we all know it's a losing situation,* but I felt obligated to clear up this issue, since it lives on forever on the Internet and I don't like being called a bigot.

Dear Emily,

I just read your review, and I would like to address a number of things that I find to be either disingenuous or just plain wrong (sometimes mildly irresponsible, and other times so wrong it borders on libel). I won't get into who had what kind of set and argue about quantifying laughs and then the qual-

---

*There seems to be a strange, double standard when it comes to attributing the emotional status of bloggers as opposed to their responders. On numerous occasions I have responded to something someone wrote about me because of a set I did, or some "racist" or "sexist" joke I made. I would defend myself or at the very least attempt to correct the impression that was given by the blogger by describing the context in which the comment took place. *Then*, and this is where the double standard takes place, someone would comment on my comment and without any thought whatsoever assume that I am "angry" or "bitter" or "thin skinned" when I made my comment. I (almost) never get as upset about that stuff as they assume.

As of right this very second I am in a good mood, my girlfriend is asleep in my bed, my dog is playing with an empty Vitamin Water bottle, and it's a beautiful day outside. I'm going over to my friends' Gavin and Emily's place for a rooftop cookout in Brooklyn later, and I'm gonna pick up some baby back ribs to throw on the grill, so I'm doing pretty good. I just truly believe that it's my place, and more pertinent to the issue, my right to defend myself against spurious comments posted by unidentified strangers who will forever remain nameless, that's all. Ironically, this itself can be perceived, and no doubt would be if I were writing this in the Comment section of a blog, as whiny and feckless. It's a frustrating and dangerous trend that does not seem to be abating. This is more than getting on a Myspace page and calling someone a fat fuck. This is lazily denigrating someone and their work based on a misperception at best, and then, once it's put out there forever, retreating into protective anonymity, much like a slug would when faced with salt, its mortal enemy!

ity of said laughs, but I take great issue with your calling me a bigot. You call me a bigot and then fail to represent truthfully what I said and ignore the context in which I said it, two very important tools in comedy. And keep in mind that the set was taped. I have it all on tape. Every word, every laugh, every pause, every quiet moment. Everything.

And Emily, if that was "the most blatant display of bigotry [you've] ever witnessed in person," then you have lived a charmed life, for sure. I think you are being hyperbolic and overdramatic, to say the least. While it's true that I made fun of Mormons and their beliefs, you completely ignored the context in which I did it. The *ENTIRE* premise of the piece was first prefaced (and this lasted over a minute) by saying that, should I ever choose to run for any kind of office, that, no matter how many good ideas I might have to improve the quality of everyone's life or implement a universal health-care plan, etc., that I could never get elected because I am an atheist. For the simple fact that I don't believe in God, most people wouldn't vote for me. I then brought up that Mitt Romney, a Mormon, had just announced his candidacy. I *then* explained that a lot of pundits thought that his prior stance in support of gay marriage might turn voters away. Then I said, "so his support of equal rights for all Americans would be the thing that made people suspicious of him, not his belief that . . ." and here is where I described the story of Joseph Smith along with side commentary about the angels' names sounding like they were members of Sha Na Na, and comments about the Freemasons, etc.

I appreciate your pointing out that there is a difference between making fun of something and attacking it, and that scientists have discovered a fine line between the two, but when you go on to say that "the greatest cultural and religious satire takes the beliefs held by a group of people and spins it to show the comedy inherent in those beliefs," you imply that I didn't "spin" it or "show" it. I disagree with you, and my tape of the set and the laughs that I was receiving are evidence that the audience (minus some, of course) disagreed with you as well. I can't (nor should I ever) assume that each audience I ever do that bit in front of is familiar with the *South Park* episode, the *Slate* article about Romney being Mormon (which I am not familiar with, but I would imagine any good journalist might find it to be an interesting subject), or even the basic tenets and history of Mormonism itself. And looking over your review I notice that I *did* in fact mention everything you cite as being so integral to the *South Park* episode.

To represent on this website that bit the way you do is damaging, if not worse. Emily, you can't simply reduce everything I said and its obvious (to most, at least) intent to merely a vitriolic, bigoted soapbox lecture wherein I just say, "This is what Mormons believe. Aren't they fucking idiots?" That is being either purposefully dishonest or at the very least lazy and irresponsible. In addition, your numerous references to how poorly I was received seem put in there to bolster your position. This just wasn't the case. Again, the set and entire evening were taped. I have the proof on tape. You have your clearly biased memory of events, which do not match reality.

Having said all that, I *do* think it's astoundingly stupid and lazy to believe in Mormonism, given it and its founder's history. I do agree with you, though, that Paul F. Tompkins had the strongest set of the night.

> Love,
> David Cross

Hmm, that wasn't very much about me at all, was it? What do you want, a memoir? Well, guess what . . .

My Memoir-to-Be

It's far too early for me to write a memoir, but barring a premature death, I most likely will. I think it's without arrogance or ego when I say that I've experienced enough interesting/scary/unique/thrilling/and heartbreaking events to warrant my writing them down and you reading them. So for now I offer this sneak peek at some of the episodes, all true, that will probably be featured in my memoir covering at least the first forty years:

- Losing my virginity to a black prostitute in a stairwell on 46th and 9th Avenue in Times Square when I was eighteen.

- Eating nothing but candy (Boston baked beans, to be exact) and chocolate powder mixed with water with my fantastically lazy and supremely irresponsible piece of useless shit of a dad in a tiny motel room/apartment in Scottsdale, Arizona, the summer I was fifteen. Needless to say, he never once found a job while I lived with him.

- Fleeing the aforementioned motel room/apartment my dad and I were staying in to skip out on several months' worth of rent that my dad got away with because he was fucking the alcoholic wife of the owner. This was just after hocking all my stuff, which barely amounted to anything.

- Arriving back at Roswell in a driveaway truck with literally one nickel left.

- Angrily/pathetically jerking off into a hole on a golf course near my apartment when I was sixteen.

- Tripping on acid with two Turkish kids who were into trance music in the middle of nowhere in the middle of Turkey. Getting paranoid and ending up the next morning on a small boat that I wound up being on for the next four days with a bunch of Australian kids.

- Being insulted by Elvis Costello backstage at a Clash concert in NYC that I miraculously got a backstage pass to while drunk off my ass on gin when I was eighteen.

- Going to the Majestic in Atlanta for some late-night drunken eats by myself, and since the place was packed and there was one table open, asking the girl ahead of me if I could sit with her at her table. She said, and I quote, "Okay, as long as you don't talk to me." Fair enough, I told her and took a seat across from her. Twenty minutes later we were making out in the parking lot. I found out she was a schoolteacher who didn't own a TV.

- Having a car screech up to me and my friend Mark while standing at the end of a gravel road in the woods in north Georgia (home of *Deliverance*) and the driver getting out, cocking a shotgun, and putting it to my chest saying, "What the hell y'all want?!!"

- Shitting my pants while talking to Tenacious D five minutes before we were supposed to start a show that I was hosting. Literally, not figuratively. I knew them already.

All this and so much more, coming to a mom-and-pop Barnes & Noble near you soon!

A Free List of Quirks for Aspiring Independent Filmmakers

THIS IS A FREE AND PARTIAL LIST OF QUIRKY PERSONALITY TRAITS, habits, or experiences for the next Diablo Cody, or Quentin Tarantino, or Miranda July, or Wes Anderson, or Jim Jarmusch, or Jason Reitman, Tom DiCillo, or fill-in-the-blank independent filmmaker, to attribute to their characters in their next film. I believe they are all worthy of inclusion. But be warned: do NOT try to use all of them in one movie! That would be an extra-crazy mindfuck of quirkdom that would unfairly sweep the Independent Spirit Awards and possibly the Best Original Screenplay Oscar!!

Born without eyelashes

Big toe bitten off by barracuda

Can't whistle

Conceived during rape

Lived in Antartica for two years

Uncle invented Ziploc bags

Precociously inventive cook at age eleven

Was a baby model

Grandfather was black

Born without an anus

Has a prehensile tail

Raised by wolves

Drinks own urine

Can play the theremin

Raped by Catholic priest, now HIV positive

Speaks fluent Mandarin

Dad was a morning zoo DJ in Buffalo, NY, named
  "Doctor Fart"

Unknowingly the rightful heir to the Danish crown

Blew off three fingers playing with blasting caps when younger

Grew up in a suite in a fancy Las Vegas casino that Dad managed

Allergic to water

Suffers from a fear of children

Knew a soldier with AIDS who died in Iraq

Clinically dead for twenty-five seconds after a car accident as
  a child

Learned how to drive when eight years old

Great aunt makes homemade absinthe

Color blind, partially deaf, and can't stop farting

Has agoraphobia

Kicked out of school for punching his/her teacher in the face

Plays the sousaphone

Plays the sousaphone in secret

Body uncontrollably gives off the odor of garlic

Allergic to pancakes

Triple-jointed

Once ate a dog on a dare

Into being peed on

Competed in the 2002 Winter Olympics

Disrupted the 2002 Winter Paralympics

Fucked Courtney Love

Was raped by Courtney Love

Has never eaten pie

Sister died in Hurricane Katrina

Was in a gay punk band in high school

Has a very valuable collection of presidential campaign
    buttons

Won a Clio award

Owns a Banksy

Has only one testicle

Left index finger is permanently fucked-up because of a copy
     machine mishap

Retarded son is an idiot savant when it comes to astrophysics

Can swear in sign language

Was once on a plane that got hijacked to Sweden. Everyone
     was okay.

Was supposed to be on one of the 9/11 planes but overslept

Lost virginity to Mom's friend, who many years later killed
     herself

Records every phone call, and has boxes and boxes of mini
     digital cassettes

Mom was a truck-stop prostitute

Has a fake kneecap

Speaks Gaelic

Can name every Carol Burnett sketch ever done

Uses a "hamburger" phone

Calls people "home skillet"

Drinks Sunny D straight from the jug

Never met a Jew

Has a third nipple

Can fart the alphabet

Went over Niagara Falls in a barrel

Knows Morse code

Great grandfather owned slaves

Once met Evel Knievel, who was mean to him

Grew up in a biosphere

Dad was a truck-stop prostitute

Dad was head of White Aryan Resistance

So poor once got only a package of Slim Jims for Christmas

Fucked a horse

Ate a tooth on a dare

Allergic to most shampoos

Has a condition called "sleepy eyes"

Has a condition called "weepy teeth"

Has a condition called "giggling ears"

Never seen *Star Wars*

Has a BB lodged in his/her neck

Was a child star in Canada

Got shit on by G. G. Allin

Got hit on by G. G. Allin

Got sat on by G. G. Allin

Only wears kilts

Lost right testicle jumping hurdles in high school

Was an integral part of making the world's largest Denver
    Omelette

Responsible for team losing the 400-meter relay in swimming at the Seoul Olympics

Semen tastes and smells like Grade-A maple syrup

Once a year reads the New Testament aloud atop Mt. Rushmore

Yells at geese

Won't poo on a plane

Only listens to reel-to-reel

Has an encyclopedic knowledge of the Gobi Desert

Graduated *summa cum laude* from M.I.T. at age ten

Like her brothers and sisters, was conceived at a NASCAR race

Father jailed for stabbing a mall Santa

Father was stabbed to death while working as a mall Santa

Survived Nagasaki but not 9/11

Does Jeff Mangum's taxes

Pilot of helicopter that decapitated Vic Morrow

Has a nostril fetish

Raised by fish

Believes *The Vagina Monologues* are real

Believes in a Sun God

Legally tried to have their astrology sign changed, which went all the way to federal court

Thought of the idea for *Survivor* but never pitched it

Came in second place at "The Living Statue" awards in Montreal in 2007

Meets with Bob Odenkirk at the Koo-Koo-Roo on Larchmont once a week

Related to the Donner Party

Quit long-time, well-paying bank CFO job to join Clown College

Has a micro-penis

Spent two months in jail for defacing the Wailing Wall with "Yankees #1!"

Jerks off to the fantasy of Will Smith jerking off to him

Aunt invented the pocket fan

As a baby, threw up on Pat Moynihan

Truly believes that he or she is a werewolf

Killed his Grandma, no one knows

Brian Eno's nephew or niece

Secretly lives in a mall

Youngest scholarship to Dartmouth ever

Shot in the ass, bullet still there

Saved the life of a retarded child

Born with no sense of smell

Saved the life of a retarded child born with no sense of smell

Can name every capital of every country in the world

Does "extra" work but solely in porn films

Spit on President Bush's food in diner once

Shit himself while getting his first blow job

Cousin was killed by Laura Bush

Killed and ate a dolphin

Was "possessed" as a child and had to be "exorcized"

Kidnapped by Farq rebels

Won $18,000 on *Wheel of Fortune*

Received a donor kidney by a murderer on death row

Has not spoken but only whistled since 9/11

Can only achieve orgasm through anal sex

Home brews their own sake

Father invented Krazy Glue but sold the rights for just five
hundred dollars

Fucked a hamburger on a dare

Has 5-20 vision

Allergic to darkness

Has a thing for astronauts

Is a white person with sickle-cell anemia

Sings in their sleep

Collects beer cans, deli meat packages, hotel "do not disturb"
  signs, toenail clippings from around the world, high school
  yearbooks, used HIV test envelopes, international audio
  recordings of people sneezing, kaddish candles, racist
  weather vanes

Grew up in a tree house

OKAY—Wait a second. These are all good and fine if you are
making an "indie" movie in the 1990s or early aughts, but that's
not gonna cut it anymore. As a culture we've become inured to so
many random quirks. If you're going to make an indie movie these
days you need to seriously up the quirk. I recommend doubling
up. You should take any of the above and combine them to make
your uninteresting movie slightly less uninteresting. For example:
Grew up in a biosphere *and* fucked Courtney Love. Or, Mom was
a truck-stop prostitute *and* was a precociously inventive cook at
age eleven. Hahaha! That's from J. T. Leroy!!!! Who it turned out
is not really real!!!!! Oh shit! Meta-quirk!!!!!!

Sitting on a Pole
Trying to Win Some Money

WELL, HERE I AM. I DO FEEL GOOD ABOUT ONE THING. ONLY three people besides me are left. And so I know that I'm gonna win something, even if it's just the Ani DiFranco tickets. I just wish it wouldn't take so long. I know that's part of the whole deal, but anyway, that's what I wish. Wish? Try pray. That's what I pray for. I don't think I've ever prayed so hard in my life. That's not true. I remember praying this hard when I was twelve and got caught with Travis Montgomery in his basement smoking cigarettes and we had our penises out and we were looking at a *Playboy*. Travis already had pubic hair then. He was the one who wanted to do the circle jerk, not me, just for the record. Wow. Why am I thinking about that stuff? I'm a grown man. Enough. Concentrate. If I can last longer than these young clowns, and I will, then I drive away with a new Chevy half-ton "Destroyer." Loaded. Easy. Larrisa thinks I'm nuts and that I won't do it. Or she thinks I *can't* do it, is more like it. Of all the things we've been through, I think that says more than everything else. She truly thinks I *can't* do it. I know I can. There's the difference right there. Hey, if nothing else I got tickets to go see a singer or a band named Ani DiFranco.

I can tell that this little shit two poles over ain't gonna make it past the hour. She's skinny, weak, and hungry and starting to get a little crazy. She's been singing some song in Arabic or something like that. Maybe Jewish? She didn't bring warm enough clothes, either, and it's supposed to snow again tonight. I was smart and ate a pound of pure fatback before getting up here. I got fat to burn! I also coated my arms with Crisco so I'll be warm, and since I was smart and got the butter-flavored kind I'll be able to sneak a snack in every once in a while. Hard to believe it's only been three days. It seems like I've been up here for a month. Outside of running out of poo room in my pants, I feel pretty good about my situation. It is boring, though. Even with all the people shouting at us. I wish they didn't put us up so high so that I could actually have a conversation with folks, or at least hear what they're saying. Five hundred feet is one of those abstract distances that you can only gauge with context. By itself you can't really conceive of it.

But here I am, a football field and a half straight up in the sky sitting on a 6 x 6 piece of reinforced plywood. I didn't count on how cold it was gonna be with the wind and all. But I need that truck. What's the second-place prize? Fuck, I can't believe I forgot. It's a year's supply of something. Noodles? Pimientos? No, it's something for around the house. Windex maybe? Whatever it is, I'm not settling for it. How much Windex do you use in a year anyway? Three or four bottles at most, right?

The funny thing is I don't even listen to Wade and the Cowgirl and hardly ever listen to the station at all. I'm not much for today's modern country. Some of it I like, but I'll take the classics any day. The Hanks, Snow and Williams. Ernest Tubb, even Jim Reeves. Those are the greats. These damn DJ's don't know when to shut up with all their guffawing and silly noises and Britney Spears jokes. I had the thing on "scan" and it landed on them talking about the truck giveaway and I locked on. Sounded simple enough. Be the last one down from their pole. Not easy, mind you, but simple. That's the key, no math or anything that had to be figured out. My kind of contest. When I told Larrisa about it she thought I'd never do it. I think that's what motivated me to go sign up even. I drove down to Duggan Chevy and did it right then and there. Now here I am, sitting on a pole trying to win some money. Or a truck, rather, but I like to look at it as free money. Because not only will I have a new truck, but I can sell my Dodge "Lacerater" to Marshal and Donna at Lotions For Less and pocket the cash. Pure profit. I wish I didn't have this song stuck in my head. I don't even know what it is. I know that Flap Montgomery sings it. I guess it's called "That's the Third Time that I've Twice Won Your Heart," cause that's the chorus part. Oh, I get it now. It's like third, twice, and the "won" part means "one," like the number one. Today's country songs do that a lot. That's what I was talking about before. I really . . . Holy shit! What the hell is this about!? There's a helicopter dropping eggs on us! What the fuck?! Good God! It's from the goddamned radio station! There's a big ol' helicopter with a Star 96.7 logo on it and . . . that's Wade! He's throwing eggs at us. What's that? It's . . . is that . . . it's the mayor! Jesus, he's got a gun! Fucking hell! Where's the Cowgirl? Is she part of this? This can't be right. What are they doing Oh sweet Jesus and Jenny! They shot the Jew girl! How do I get down from here? Wait, no. Fuck that! This is a test. I ain't quittin'. I need that truck.

Concentrate, goddammit. Now, there's just three of us left. Ow! Fucking hell! Is that pepper spray? And . . . pineapples? They're throwing pineapples at us? There's no way this was mentioned in that contract thing we signed. Why didn't I read that thing? Note to self: Read contracts thoroughly from now on! Oh! Someone is lowering a rope? Thank God. Or is this a trick? Oh, God! The Korean War vet just jumped off! Oh God, oh God. He just jumped on his own. Hey, just two left! I'll at least get the window cleaner.

Oh, come on now, I gotta stick this out. There's a blimp, too? Why is there a blimp? That rope is . . . not a rope! It's a fucking snake! Shit! Ahhhh, it's on me!! I don't get this?! Why???? Get it off me! The blimp is opening up! There's a cargo door opening! Oh, thank sweet cousin Jesus! I'm being rescued! This must be one of those prank reality shows! Ha ha! I get it! The blimp is . . . wait, is that an old Australian man's flabby ass sticking out of it? Is that . . . Oh, my God!!!

Didja Know?

Crazy True Fun True True Facts

Eggs are the only food that are both nutritious and mathematically impossible!

If the Sears Tower in Chicago was made entirely out of buttons, it would be the world's tallest building made entirely out of buttons!

Butte, Montana, is home to the world's second largest nickel!

It takes more muscles and longer to say, "No, thank you" than it does to not!

Children are America's future and the elderly are America's past and forty-two-year-olds are its present!

The word *fucktwit* was coined by Harriet Tubman after a shitty bath!

In Georgia, it is illegal for a man to secretly find another man attractive!

The best way to get cum stains out of your hair is with simple peanut butter and very complex soda water!

Although we are taught that blood is thicker than water, on the moon, the reverse is true!

If birds could swim, that'd be awesome! Also, they'd most likely be penguins!

Contrary to the common belief that Mexico is home to more explosive diarrhea than any other nation, surprisingly it's actually Austria!

You cannot legally fold something more than twice in Canada!

The only two chemicals found in Dippin' Dots, the unpopular ice cream, are polyhexachlorine and deliciousness!

A quick, and surefire way to tell if you are psychic is whether you are susceptible to coincidence!

In China, it is illegal to try to change your astrology sign.

In the great state of Alaska, fetuses have exactly as many rights as Tonya Gumm, a sixteen-year-old who was raped by Dupree Bellsmith, a retired pipe fitter with the local 173 and registered sex offender who was recently released from prison early due to overcrowding, and actually slightly more than D'nesh Bhowmik, a recent émigré and tech support worker for the United Nations!

I Hate America!
or, I Hate America?

I'VE BEEN ACCUSED OF "HATING AMERICA." NOT DIRECTLY, BUT by association. Because I don't agree with the majority of pundits and radio talk show hosts and various columnists and bloggers in the mass media—that is to say, on the right wing side of things. But I *do* agree (most of the time) with the diametrically philosophically opposed on the left of that media spectrum. I like reading Paul Krugman and Greg Sargent and Markos Moulitsas. I usually feel enlightened and not merely pandered to. I try my best to be aware of easy emotional manipulation. And I do enjoy listening to Sean Hannity and Mark Levin and Rush Limbaugh but mostly for the entertainment value. For instance, I remember once hearing Sean Hannity talk about exorcisms in the Catholic Church (this is for real). A fundamental part of the conversation was the tacitly understood idea that exorcisms were legitimate. Imagine! A grown man treating the idea of exorcising the "Devil" out of some mentally ill elderly woman as a real thing. Crazy!* You're not gonna find crazy gold like that on Air America.

Personally, and I am being absolutely honest here, I have never felt like I hated America. Not even in my acid-dropping, Hunter S. Thompson–reading, angry punk-listening days. I would even say that maybe, just maybe, I love America. Much like the conflicted love one might have for an abusive parent or caretaker with a bipolar condition making them capable of true empathy and magnanimous compassion while meting out cold, unsympathetic, financial "tough love" lessons. My feelings about my country are in the spirit of caring about a fucked-up friend whose condition you hope doesn't get so bad that they end up on A&E's *Intervention*. I do have a number of negative observations and complaints about America's domestic and foreign policies and what I would hope against hope would be seen as legitimate questions and/or constructive criticism and not virulent anger spewed and screamed

---

*Side note rhetorical question: Why does the Devil only seem to inhabit the very young or old? In other words, weak people? Why wouldn't the Devil inhabit the body of Arnold Schwarzenegger or someone like that? Then he could not only tear the heads off of his enemies in true "Hulk" style but also pass legislation outlawing crosses and holy water, or whatever it is that makes the Devil scared. Holy water, right? Isn't that what turns the Devil into a shaking, quivering mess, retreating in the corner while pissing himself in fear? I know that if you sprinkle some tap water from Tel Aviv and wave a small metal sculpture of Jesus on the cross at him, that he nearly shits himself in fear and general discomfort. The Devil. Right, Sean Hannity? That's what your religion teaches you, yes? Why would anybody in their right mind be scared of such an ineffective Devil? The Catholic Devil is an even bigger pussy than Ralph Nader. And I say the Catholic Devil because he doesn't really exist in other cultures. You never hear of the Devil inhabiting the body of Mrs. Rabinowitz in North Brook, Illinois. Or Lee Po Hung of Guangdong Province. That's because they don't believe in that kind of devil. The Devil only shows up and does harm if you believe in him. That's how it works, so perhaps the best way to get rid of him is to stop believing in him. Sort of like a reverse Tinker Bell. Holy shit! That's a fight I would love to see! Satan vs. Tinker Bell! Pay-per-view on Imax in 3-D!!!

from a clinically insane lunatic fringe lefty, communist moon bat or whatever invective Michelle Malkin is using today.

But maybe I'm wrong. Maybe I really *do* hate America. I mean, could all of these people who make these accusations be wrong? The odds are against it. They can't *all* be wrong, could they? The answer is, of course, "No," judging by their own criteria. They aren't wrong. Ever. They have never been wrong about anything. Not once! Not even once. They've "misspoken" several times where they've said one word but meant something else entirely and weren't even aware of it until it was pointed out later. Their words have been taken out of context. And occasionally what they've said has been unfortunately "misinterpreted," but that's not really their fault. In the guise of their public persona, they have never made a *genuine* apology or, having the valuable benefit of hindsight, changed their position about a polemic event unless it was cajoled by some vague, begrudging idea of propriety. And if they've never felt the need to apologize or at the very least take responsibility for those statements, then clearly, they must be right. I mean they have to be right . . . right? And their counterparts on the left have categorically apologized for past incorrect facts and projections. I've heard or read the apologies, I know they exist. So, if those who are *always* correct say that I hate America, and the people that are accused of hating America but say that they don't *but* have admitted to being wrong about certain things, then, ipso facto, I must hate America!

Again, I didn't think that I did hate America, but now that I know that it must be true, even though I don't think it is, it would be highly irresponsible of me, not to mention traitorous, to just sit back and do nothing. I need to explore what this is all about. How did I come to hate America, and what can be done about it? At the very least I should identify the ways that I am an immediate danger to the welfare of this country that I, and all of my family and friends, call home.

Okay, we are taught from a young age that *hate* is a strong word and shouldn't be tossed around lazily. Since I learned this lesson I have tried to reserve the emotion of hate for people like Adolf Hitler and Eva Braun, Osama Bin Laden and his fine, fine lady, whoever she may be, or Bull Connor and Timothy McVeigh or people like that. I may say that I "hate" Whoopie Goldberg, but I don't really hate her, that's just exaggerated hyperbole to express how extremely annoying, unfunny, and sanctimonious I find her. Which is slightly ironic because I have been accused of the same things I just accused her of, so one might think we'd be BFFs. But no, I fucking hate her (not really *hate*, though).

So, with a better understanding of what hate really means (absolute revulsion, abhorrence, *extreme* dislike) and what it doesn't mean (annoyance, frustration, displeasure, someone whose career and reputation as a "funny" woman is completely unjustified given the lack of a single funny, original thing ever being uttered), let's explore my hatred of America.

Let's start here: From the deductions made from the above information, I know that when Ann Coulter, or Rush Limbaugh, or Laura Ingraham and their millions upon millions of listeners who agree with them say that I, or my like-minded ilk, are traitorous, it means that we are. This is irrefutable and thus closed to discussion. It is, in other words, a fact. This puts me in an epic conundrum, for I would like to live here for the rest of my life and someday raise and eat a family here. Wait—just raise, not eat. I live in New York City, which, to me, is the greatest city in the history of ever. I truly love it here and not one day goes by that I don't have occasion to reflect on this. But as we all know, New York City is in New York State. One of the states that comprises the United States of . . . America! Great! Now what?!

It stands to reason that as someone who hates America (like Mohamed Atta, and the sixteen other Saudis who kamakazied planes into the World Trade Center and Pentagon but not the one over

Pennsylvania because that was shot down—sorry, Todd), my continued presence here is a security risk. I don't know how much of a risk, though. That should be left to the experts in National Security Risk Assessment. Those experts being amongst others the aforementioned pundits and their brethren, Neal Boortz, Bill O'Reilly, William Bennett, James Dobson, Michael Savage, etc., etc.

So freedom, liberty, and justice for all (coincidentally, the names of my three dogs) and I are at odds. Even if I say we are not. Even if I think we are not. According to them, I would rather live in some theocracy with just one ruling class, being bombarded by a twenty-four-hour propaganda machine in place that effectively demeans dissent and marginalizes those who don't pray to the country's approved god? Hey . . . wait a minute!!!

Heaven!

ACCORDING TO THE SHEPARD INSTITUTE IN SLILLFORTH, NEW Mexico, as of this date there are over 2 trillion people in Heaven right now. Wow! That's a lot of people! True fact: if you laid 2 trillion people head to toe and then wrapped them all in foil, they would circle the earth upwards of tons of times. The Shepard Institute received a grant for this study from a conservative "think" tank based in Washington, DC, that studies new ways to pay for justifying its existence. They commissioned the study after a prior study, funded by the very same think tank, showing that America is primarily a Judeo-Christian country (although not so much the Judeo part*) whose laws are founded upon those ideals. Now, let's get back to the figure 2 trillion. This is based on a combination of all denominations that believe in the existence of Heaven. This includes religions that have been in existence

---

*2.6 percent of America is Jewish. Doesn't it seem like so much more? I guess they're just really good at getting on TV, or maybe it's because the really religious ones are so unbelievably annoying and rude.

prior to AD 1 that may have believed in the concept, no matter how vague and undefined, of an eternal reward waiting for the followers of said religions, after their mortal life on this earth was ended. For the purpose of this study, all heavens have been amalgamated into one heaven, which must share at least these three basic tenets:

1. Heaven is a reward for those who live and abide by the basic ideals as stated by their respective religions regardless of direct contradiction of another's religion, which will also see its followers going to the same heaven. In other words, if one was a member of say, the Church of Revenge, whose members were instructed to take the lives of doctors or nurses who perform or advise on abortions in order to win passage to Heaven, they would be in Heaven alongside Unitarians, who believe that one shouldn't kill another human being under any circumstances but should only help and aid in distress, and thereby might, in turn, help another attain the aforementioned abortion.

2. Admission to Heaven is decided upon by an all-knowing supreme being of undetermined origin and physicality, who has complete knowledge of the entirety of one's life actions, inner thoughts, and intent. This being also has the ability to contextualize each action and thought within time, place, situation, cultural understanding of one's surroundings, one's chemical makeup, physical well-being, as well as forces of nature without.

3. Heaven itself in its physical description is either so breathtaking and awe inspiring as to be literally be-yond description by mere human language, or the

exact opposite—able to be described by the following words or their foreign-language (i.e., not English)
counterparts: *majestic, regal, royal, grand, stately,
imposing, grandiose, magnificent, daunting, inspiring, remarkable,* and *extraordinary.* Heaven must
be said to be a place where "God shall wipe away
all tears from their eyes; and there shall be no more
death, neither sorrow, nor crying, neither shall there
be any more pain: for the former things are passed
away" (Revelation 21:4).

It should be ascribed with physical traits in topography, ge-
ology, temperate climate systems, ecosystems, zoology, distribution of attributable race, and basic geography that are familiar to
humans depending on where they live and their immediate familiar surroundings—i.e., a Baptist who grew up in a holler in the
foothills of the Smoky Mountains without television or computers
would believe in a heaven much like the pristine woods he or she
grew up in and know only of, while an inner-city Muslim who
grew up in Beirut might know of a much different, albeit as equally
beautiful, heaven resembling the biblical Golan Heights.

With a 3% +/– margin of error, the heavens include, but are
not limited to: Calvanists, Baptists, Protestants, Lutherans, Meth-
odists, Amish, Sumerians, Hittites, Jehovah's Witnesses, Roman
Catholics, Greek Orthodox, and Mormons. So basically a Christian heaven. There are probably not too many Japanese or Chinese
in Heaven. I mean, they came to it late in the game. I wonder, is
there a special section for racists in Heaven? I mean racist children
that have never broken any of the Ten Commandments, been good
kids, accepted Jesus but died early only knowing what their racist
family yelled. Do they have to hang out with all the mud people in
Heaven? Or is there a special South Boston Public Housing project
just for them?

What if, according to the Catholic concept of Heaven, that due to such stringent rules and the impossibility of maintaining purity in thought and deed, that only seven people were in Heaven, and they're all bored now.

Mormons are my favorite religion, I think. Anybody who can convince millions of people that an angel appeared before him at four different occasions throughout one night and told him that under a tree in Upstate NY there were some gold tablets that ONLY HE could unearth and interpret (which would happen by looking into his hat, and then God would tell him what is what) has got my vote for President of Fools (not to be confused with the pope, who is President of Scaredy Cats).

It's my observation that religion, at its best, is a benign waste of time. At its worst, of course, it can slaughter thousands and ruin generation after generation of lives—causing, through its un-rivaled "tough love" stance, millions to take their own lives due to an imposed unbearable shame. Count me in. Sounds like a fun bunch of fun. But religion is not supposed to be "fun." Or is it? Take a look at the cover of any *Watchtower* magazine that a Jeho-vah's Witness may be lucky enough to throw away after they wake up from their insane delusion. Look at it! That looks like plenty of fun! Standing on the back of a tiger while picking ripe fruit in a bucolic, pastoral setting with a pretty Chinese lady and black man from Kenya while petting a lion! Awesome! What about the whirl-ing Dervishes? The Sufis who twirl around until they hyperven-tilate, which was a cheap way to get high before chemicals came along? Fun!! And we've all seen *Fiddler on the Roof* and that scene at the end of *Schindler's List*, too. Fun times.

But what about the little babies who died before getting cleansed of their sins, you might ask? What about their fun? Who's going to speak out for them? Try me! I'll do it!

The Five People You Meet in Limbo

I RECENTLY WAS STUCK IN THE SHREVEPORT, LOUISIANA, AIRPORT suffering through numerous delays of my trip back to 2008 and *away* from Shreveport. I had exhausted nearly everything readable save for a back issue of *Yachting Monthly* magazine, which I had already committed to memory. Mitch Albom's celebrated book *The Five People You Meet in Heaven* was the only thing left that I hadn't read. So, even though I suspected that I wouldn't care for it, I picked it up to read. Twenty minutes later, when I had finished, I got to thinking. There's Albom's book, Gender Tripp's *The Five People You Meet in Hell* (three of them are Dick Cheney), Dr. Pat Nunking's *The Five People You Meet While Reading The Five People You Meet in Heaven*, Su Tsing's *The Five Scented Candles You Will Enjoy in Heaven*, and Peter Mayhew's *The Five Star Wars Fans You Will Meet in Hell*. But where was the book for all the babies that died before they could be baptized and know God's sweet redemption from sins they had not yet had the opportunity to commit? This hardly seemed fair. Where was Sean Hannity in this time of need? Is that Roman

Catholic too focused on promoting the legitimacy of sanctioned exorcists to ignore the plight of the innocent three-week-olds who are living at the edge of hell? So, with the trillions of innocents floating around in space, I dedicate these lists to them.

The Five People You Meet in Limbo

Rubeun Vandalhavenn, a Dutch architect who died in 1838 of lumbago. He is a bit of a dick.

Afshar Muhammed Timor from Kandahar. A tribal sheep-herder from last week.

Jeannette Dunwoody, a housewife and mother of three from Cobb County, GA. She died in 1981 from complications arising from a medical procedure to remove her eye fat.

Billy Preston. Yeah, that Billy Preston.

Grrk, a nomadic hunter and gatherer from 19,939 BC. Died of old age at twenty-two years. He is virtually useless but provides comic relief while you wait to get into Heaven.

The Five Snacks You Have While You're in Limbo

Tewilliger's Fudge 'n' Honey Crinkle Cakes. A sugary sweet taste of a seaside British yesteryear.

Tom's of Maine All Natural Cinnamint Toothpaste. This is actually a snack for some people. Seriously.

Waltman's cherry-covered overalls. A delicious pant.

Tom's Bottom of the Barrel, Powder-Flavored 'Tato Chips.

Reiling's Swiss Herbal Rocks 'n' Dirty.

The Four Salt & Pepper Shakers You Will Use in Limbo

The ones that look like Laurel and Hardy

The ones that look like cows

The battery-operated grinders currently featured in *SkyWays* magazine

The ones that look like Raggedy Anne and Andy

The Eleven Vitamins You Will Have in Limbo

B12 (obviously!!)

C

K

C+

D–

Niacin (duh!)

A

E

Zinc (surprise!)

B_6

St. John's Wort (not a vitamin really, but still . . .)

The Eight Greetings You Will Hear in Limbo

'Sup.

Shalom.

'Allo, guv.

Mushi-Mushi.

Duuuude!

Buenos dias.

Ugh.

Hey, you're that guy from the thing!

The Fourteen Twelves You Will Six in Limbo

Malcolm X

"Where's the beef?"

One thousand four hundred and three

The Who's *Live at Leeds*

Connie Chung

PooBerries

Seattle

Bianca Jagger

Mylanta Chewables

A patch of Kentucky bluegrass

"Yahtzee!"

Les Savy Fav

Ideas for T-shirts to
Be Sold at Urban Outfitters

WE'VE ALL BEEN TO URBAN OUTFITTERS, SO DON'T TRY TO bullshit me. If you insist on lying and saying that you haven't, then I'll describe it. It's a store that is targeted to "hipsters," but no real hipster would be caught dead in there unless they wanted that one cool shower curtain that has pictures of turn-of-the-century French nudie postcards that no one else carries anymore so you have no choice but to go there, right? Most of the stuff there is not too offensively lame. Mostly that kitschy shit that girls who dye one small streak of their hair purple or pink or some other Manic Panic color think is cute. Genetalia-shaped ice-cube trays or mood rings, or Che Guevara–scented candles. Shit like that. But the one part of Urban Outfitters I really take issue with is their line of faux vintage "hip" T-shirts. They are sooooo un-funny and obvious, and only a total tool into 3 Doors Down who still drinks vodka and Red Bull and is starting to seriously get into UFC fighting would think they were cool for wearing one. So, with that in mind, I have some suggestions for the next line of T-shirts to be sold at Urban Outfitters. Just sneak them in there amongst the regular ones. Maybe someone will buy one by mistake and get beat up in a bar.

I Brake for Fucking

Punch Me, I'm Pregnant

Don't Bother Me, I'm a Pedophile

I Have to Go to the Bathroom

My Other Shirt Is Funnier

This shirt was made by slave labor and sold for a 1,200% markup

Look at what I think is interesting!

Oklahoma Is for Racists!

My Other Car Is a Porsche

Penny for your thoughts? Are you fucking nuts? Try ten bucks for my thoughts is more like it! This is America!

Don't Blame Me! I Voted for Christ!

God Is My Enabler

I Fucked Jesus

Mohammed told me he thinks his followers are lunatics

Hugh Hefner's got nothing on Joseph Smith!

My God can beat up your God

Thank God for Autistic Children

In Anticipation of Reading This Right Now

PART OF TODAY'S MODERN BOOK-SELLING PROCESS IS THE "BOOK tour," in which the author or a suitable preapproved surrogate* travels to various bookstores around the country and occasional Canadian province and reads excerpts from his or her book that is being sold mere inches away. Depending on the author's comfort with public speaking, this can be either a frightening and excruciating chore or another in a rarely ending series of ego-inflating exercises happily sponsored by Absolut Vodka. I am of the latter camp. I was trained professionally at the Helmsdale Institute for Audience Ignoring, and that makes me uniquely qualified contractually to help sell this book by reading from it in places like [fill in the name of the city you are currently in here].

Before I continue and read from the book and then have the raffle for the set of outdoor throw pillows designed by Asconti, let me just say that [fill in the name of the city you are currently in here]

---

*If I am not able to make it, then the State of New York has vested Dame Judi Dench to speak in my stead.

is really cool! I love the history and culture here! I can't believe that that lady who did that thing lived at that house just down the road! As someone who has traveled all over the world, whether shooting pheasant with the Earl of Duke in Shroppingham or enjoying "Untouchables" eyeball soup with the Rani of Kharmuknan, I can easily say that [fill in the name of the city you are currently in here] is the most wonderful place I've ever visited. I wish I could live here! God!! Have you checked out the Bed Bath & Beyond here?! I've seen a bunch of those, but man, this one . . . wow! Seriously, I'm not getting paid by them or anything (**NOTE TO EDITOR: SEE ABOUT GETTING PAID BY THEM! Also, the socks need discussion!!!**), but you should check out the towel section, tons of great shit cheap! I can see why you'd want to stay here and never leave. Not even to take a bit of time to visit other parts of the world.

Well, enough about your lovely town and its convenient access to various products that you feel you need, let's read some of this insulting book! I mean, *interesting* book! Haha. I said "insulting" by mistake. Slip of the tongue there. Just a Freudian slip. Wait! No, not Freudian, that would imply that I subconsciously felt that this book is insulting when it is not. It's *me* who can be insulting . . . and occasionally cynical and condescending, sure, but not the book. Arrrgh! I've got to stop believing my own press! I'm not some grumpy Gen-X Andy Rooney. I'm barely even Gen-X! By, like, a month or something. I missed being a Baby Boomer by about five minutes. I sooooo want to be a Baby Boomer! Anyway, the book is great, I'm proud of it! I wrote a book, for fuck's sake! What have you ever done? Tipped generously at a Hooters in Playa del Carmen? Fixed your elderly neighbor's satellite dish? Made a kid? Who gives a shit? I can make a kid no one but you and maybe a handful of babysitters will ever give a shit about. I can do that with just my cock and a roofie. If contributing yet another human monkey to this overcrowded world to do nothing with their precious gift of life other than spend it predictably consuming precious resources and blogging about how they think that *American Idol* is starting to lose it, so they can then grow up to make another unnotable Wal-Mart greeter—if that makes you some sort of hero, then call 911 and tell them I give up.

Okay, let's get to the good stuff, the reason we're all here! The chance to sit in a room with someone who's been on your television box because that's so fascinating to the dull and uninspired. What!? I didn't mean that. I don't even know any of you. I'm sure that for the most part, at least half of you aren't a bunch of boring, complacent, slightly overweight people haunted by the constant nagging of "what-if"s and "should I have"s. Okay, okay, sit down. Please, I apologize . . . to God . . . for you. No! No, sorry. That was a stupid joke. I don't even believe in God. I don't know what's come over me. It's been a long tour. I ran out of Zoloft back in Jacksonville. Plus I was just in Jacksonville. I am having some more Zoloft airlifted in, so as soon as it gets here I'll be okay. Just pretend I'm my own evil twin or something. Just until the Zoloft gets here and then we'll be right as rain. At least I can take a pill and get better—you lot are stuck in your shitty uneventful lives unless one of you turns Goth and decides to check out Portland or something. Oh my lord! Please forgive me. It's been a very long day. I had to do three morning radio shows and *FOX & Friends* at the crack of dawn. Have you ever seen *FOX & Friends*? How? Why? These are grown-ups saying this nonsense! The inanity of that show is matched only by its meaninglessness. One of Amy Winehouse's collapsed veins has more weight than that show.

All right, good. Now we're back to something we can all agree on, the outrageous *FOX & Friends*. They honestly look like they truly believe what they are saying! Can you imagine getting drunk and hanging out with the three of them? I can. We'd have margs at the Yupplebee's and I would drink them all under the table and then I'd probably find myself tying them up and burying them up to their necks in the middle of the projects in Detroit. That sounds fun, actually. Let me linger on that image for one sweet second. Mmmmm. Oh, that's good. Woah! There's Steve Douchey being shat upon by one of the neighborhood kids! Oh! Hahahaha! Mmmm, yeah . . . that's the way I like it . . . like that. Yeah, get that spot over there . . . good. Mmmmmm, oh . . . I'm gonna cum. Don't stop shitting . . . unh. Sputter. Snore.

Gay Canada

as written by Kenny Dupree Hester

YOU'VE PROBABLY READ ALL ABOUT THIS BY NOW, BUT ENOUGH time has passed that I feel like I want to tell my side of the story, so here goes. There are three things you should know about my aunt Patricia (really my great-aunt, but we just call her aunt): One, she is a devout, constantly churchgoing Baptist. Two, she is quiet, and even timid. And three, she hates the cold. That's why it was so surprising last year when Aunt Patricia casually announced to our family and friends that she had sold all her belongings except for her three favorite Thomas Kincaid paintings (*Summer's Light Light, The House by the Stream with Horses Nearby It,* and *When an Angel Finds a Wallet*) and gave all the money to a shady group in the woods who used it to purchase a number of semiautomatic weapons and a barn on a big plot of land in Upstate NY. This of course was met with confusion as not one of us could ever remember her making a joke, let alone laughing. Although my sister says she saw her laugh when an elderly man was running for a bus that pulled away without him right as he got up to the door. And I guess she did love watching *Mama's Family,* she just never laughed at it.

It was clear she was being dramatic in the way she was parsing out the information. My mom knew enough to take her seriously but could do nothing but wait on the phone patiently for Aunt Patricia to fill in the blanks. Eventually she explained that she and a handful of members of her church group, "The Guardians of the Realm of Good," in Henry, Georgia, were planning to move to New Harriden in New York state, a small rural town bordering Canada. There they would form the "New, New Minutemen" (as they referred to themselves), made up of various "intercessors" from other like-minded church groups across the country who would keep watch over America's border and defend it from newly married Canadian homosexual couples who might be trying to sneak into the country to advance their homosexual agenda. They were very, very serious.

Aunt Patricia was known for being a bit "lost" when it came to matters both social and practical in her life. She was always searching for a clique to belong to. Whether it was something as small as a group of new friends she'd try to make through a sewing circle or book club or her unsuccessful attempt at a "Raisin of the Month" party she tried to get going. Sometimes it was something much more involved, like joining every church in a fifty-mile radius at once, she never seemed to either have enough friends to satisfy her or couldn't maintain them as friends.

Before being newly re-re-baptized in "The Guardians of the Realm of Good," Aunt Patricia was a member of "The Church of the Good Deed," which she joined after leaving "The Shield of the Wrath of Christ," an offshoot of "The Church of Christ and Friends," which had split from "The Church of the All-Powerful Redeemer" in 1982 over its use of the phrase "befouled menstrual blood of the filthier half." That had been included in a screed written by Delmont Ralston, the church's personable leader, who was killed in 1985 when he tried to eat a lightning bolt. Before she started to attend all of these different churches, Aunt Patricia was involved in our local neighborhood theater group, helping to stage inoffensive musicals like *Parrump! Oh Boy! What Fun!* and *The Great Missouri Whistle Days Discovery*. We didn't really spend too much time with her, as my mom clearly had nothing in common with her and, in fact, felt she was a near constant source of annoyance with her corrections and holier-than-thou attitude. That was okay with my sisters and me, as none of us particularly liked her, either.

I remember one Christmas, she gave all of us Confederate scrip, which is worthless unless you have a working time machine. Another time she gave the three of us kids compost, lecturing us on the "divine sanctity which has been granted in the compost through the gift of God and emanates from within, purifying all who touch it." Like I said before, she wasn't any fun. She didn't even approve of water-skiing, saying once that it was "an activity that could only be sanctioned by Satan himself." Aunt Patricia was married to my great-uncle Abraham, who I don't remember too much about, since he died when I was young. I do remember he smoked a pipe and had jackets with patches on the elbows that smelled like old mustard and that he had gross, hairy ears. Really hairy, though, not just a little bit, but like, all hair. It made me think that ear hair must have hurt because otherwise he'd just cut it off. Then, when I got older and learned that it didn't hurt, it actually made me a little sick to my stomach every time I'd think of him after that.

On the day we found out, my sisters, Abby and Jenny, and I were out back in the woods lazily playing some kind of freeze-tag game in which the rules were being made up and changed as we went along. My mom came outside with the phone in her hands. She seemed upset and yelled to us with the kind of tone she only used for bad news or when she had one of her stomachaches but didn't want to show it. Without even waiting for a response, Mom yelled at us to all come inside. My sister Abby started whining about how we just got out there and we were in the middle of the game, and Mom yelled at Abby to get inside NOW and went back in, letting the screen door slam shut (which she HATED whenever we did it) behind her. Abby started again with her whining: "But, Mom, you said . . ." I hit Abby in the head with a crabapple and told her to shut up. When she said she was gonna tell on me I said, "Go right ahead. Mom hates you right now for crying when she told you to get inside. She'll probably give me a dessert reward 'cause I made you quit." That shut her up, and she tromped into the kitchen behind me.

"Hey, guys, sit down at the table."

We could all sense bad news was coming.

"Your aunt Patricia passed on last night." There was silence from all of us. I felt like I should say something out of a vague sense of respect, even though I didn't care and I knew my sisters didn't care, either. And I suspected that Mom didn't, either, but maybe this was one of those grown-up things where God just makes you somehow magically care when you have to.

"Oh," I said and tried to look sad. "How did she die? Was it peaceful?"

My mom opened the freezer and took out some ice pops.

"She was involved in a shoot-out with some FDA agents and was shot in the head and chest over a dozen times." That seemed funny to me, and I laughed, and my mom shot me an annoyed but understanding look, like someone who was in on the joke but didn't want the other people in the room to know.

"Does everyone want ice pops?"

My two sisters raised their hands, and Jenny asked what my mom meant.

"Well, sweetheart," my mom said as she sat down and gave out the ice pops. "Remember how Aunt Patricia moved up to that farm in New York, the one near the border with Canada? Where that nice man paid for that big, nineteen-hour Canadian fireworks display that Aunt Patricia told you about? And remember how she told us all before she went that she was going to do the Lord's work and how even if something bad happened that she would get to go to Heaven where seventy white angels awaited her with baskets of apple fritters and hot cocoa?"

Jenny nodded and took her ice pop.

"Well, that's what happened."

"She's with Jesus and the angels having cocoa?"

"That's right, honey."

"I wanna have hot cocoa with the angels!" Abby said.

"Me, too!" said Jenny quickly and even more emphatically. As if not saying so in time would disqualify her from going to Heaven.

"You can't have cocoa with angels until you're dead, stupid. You have to wait." I looked to my mom to see if what I said and even what I was doing was the right thing. She had her back to us and was staring inside at the open freezer. After a bit she closed it and turned around. "Kenny's right." Then, in a surprise to all of us, she smiled and said those magic words: "Hey, who wants to go to Dairy Queen?" We all jumped up and yelled, "We do! We do!"

When we got to Dairy Queen, I ordered the Nut Buster Parfait which is the only thing I've ever gotten there. It's my all-time favorite thing ever. We had just gotten our stuff and sat down when the TV that was on in the corner up by the ceiling had one of those "Breaking News" things with all the explosions and space-war sounds. There was a photo of Aunt Patricia that I hadn't seen before. She was in an army uniform and she had a black eye. They were talking about all these people being killed up in NY and how she was from here and that's why they were showing her picture. Mom gasped and stared silently and then, like she was shocked or something, started to quickly gather our desserts and us and told us to get into the car. But I pretended I left my free *Pirates of the Carribean* figurine I got with the sundae on the seat and went back inside to listen. The news lady called the church that she was with a terrorist group and said that they were kidnapping gays who went to Canada to get gay married there and "unmarry-ing" them by force. They raised funds going across the border into Canada and buying up lots of prescription medicines, which were a lot cheaper up there, and then selling them online back in NY for five times as much money. That's how they afforded all their guns and things. Plus the guns were super cheap at the Wal-Mart where they lived. I guess one of the gays had escaped and told the police about it, and that's when they had the shoot-out.

Pretty soon my mom figured out what I was doing and came in really angry. I lied and told her I just remembered it was in the car, but she saw right through that. She told me we'd talk when we got home. We drove home in silence except for Abby singing a song under her breath about all the things she saw out her window. When we got back home, Mom put on the TV for Jenny and Abby to watch and took me by the hand down into the basement. She did the "shhh" thing where you put your finger to your lips mean-ing "Don't say anything." She went to the windowsill at the far end near the boiler and stood on her tippy-toes and felt around on the upper ledge of it. She finally got a key from on top and, without waiting for me, walked around to where the lawn mower and all the garden equipment was. She moved it all over to one side, and I realized for the first time ever that there was a small door there. It had a rusty old lock on it. I never even knew there was a door there!! She unlocked it, again did the "shhhh" thing, and opened it up. It smelled like raw pancake batter. I mean it wasn't that, but that's what it smelled like. My mom closed her eyes, took a deep breath, and then sort of flung herself in. I tried to

END PART ONE (idrinkforareason.com/gaycanadapartII)

You'll Never Guess!!!

HOLY SHIT! GUESS WHAT? REMEMBER BEFORE AT THE BEGINNING of the book when I was imagining that I would be invited to all these wonderful author parties? Well, I've just been invited to attend a party this weekend! No shit! It's at the mid-summer home of Charmin Killington (of the Willowbrook Killingtons). It sounds exactly like one of those "literary" parties I was fantasizing about earlier. Wow. Now I will get to see firsthand what it's like and not have to rely on my adorably jaded speculations. And I of course will write about it. In fact, it should follow this sentence directly:

Yes!!! I'm here! I arrived by Filipino butler arms to the house after taking the griffin-pulled hansom cab from the outer moat. This house is fucking HUGE! The pool house's pool toy's storage room's wine cellar is easily as big as the apartment I grew up in. I was greeted by one of the Puerto Rican eunuchs stationed around the entrance. He sang a song of fierce bidding wars as he dropped gilded lilies at my feet. I felt at once self-conscious and oddly liberated. "This is my new life," I thought.

"I like it." I involuntarily started to imagine how others saw me. I would vacillate from Dickensian street urchin with a smudge of soot and rotten lettuce around my mouth wearing week-old newsiepapers for shoes, to your basic Ivy League nerd who has benefited from a scholarship that your great-uncle, the mustard baron, established. A severe-looking waitress passed by carrying flutes of champagne with small black pearls floating on top. In a deft mix of balance and classlessness, I took two, shooting one down and handing it back. With my mouth closed, I motioned for the waitress to stay and parted my lips to reveal the pearl between my front teeth. I bent slightly and said, "A beautiful black pearl, for a beautiful black pearl," although because I couldn't really close my lips all the way it came out more as, "A uteful lack earl or a uteful lack earl." "What?" she coquettishly replied. "A uteful lack earl or a . . ." I lightly spit the pearl onto her tray. "A beautiful black pearl for a beautiful black pearl, is what I was saying." She looked at me with what some might mistake as violent contempt but what I could clearly see was lustful frustration. "I'm not black," she said as she masterfully "pretended" to walk away while walking away. I was in!! Newly imbued with confidence, I swaggered over to a table of dandies and rifled through one of the ladies' purses. I took eighty dollars, making a point of showing that I was still leaving her with most of her money. So as not to appear impolite, I sat down. "Hi, I'm David Cross from television and now books. Well, *a* book. Singular."

"Oh, yes. A humor book, right?"

"Well, let's hope so. It's supposed to be."

"Well then, you should be at that table over there. That's the humor table. This is Puppies and Fish."

I looked around and realized that the entire party had been arranged so that each table represented a type of book. Seated at my table were Jeff Foxworthy, Dave Barry, Cathy Guisewite, Ann

Coulter, and Rabbi Shmuley Boteach, amongst others. We were in between the "Yes, You Can, Goddammit!" table and the "Kids Are Nature's Crybabies" table. I took the hat off of the gentleman to my left, put it on, and then doffed it to the table before giving it back to its rightful owner. "A thousand pardons." I smiled and moseyed over to the humor table.

HOLY SHIT! Alert!!

I was obviously making all this up, but now I have some real news to report! So, as I'm sitting here writing (currently in my East Village apartment on break from shooting a movie—that's right, you heard me, a MOVIE!) I got a phone call from a number I didn't recognize. I let the machine get it, and it's from a woman named "Leslie Tietalbaum" (I'm guessing the spelling of her name) who works at a public relations firm here in NY. She left a message that I was invited to a charity event taking place upstairs at the Saks Fifth Avenue store in midtown. It's in a little over three weeks from now. My invite is due to the book that I'm writing right this very second and you are reading (in the present *and* future!) right this very second. So there you go. Fiction gets replaced by nonfiction. Fantasy, by fact. I could waste some time conjecturing, seriously, what it will be like, but then you'd have to trust that I didn't go back and rewrite it to make myself look impressively prescient. And I don't believe that I have earned your trust yet. So I am going to stop right here and whatever follows this sentence will be my "reporting" on what (honestly) took place at the aforementioned charity thing.

OKAY! Just got back from the "Evening in Gold to Benefit the Evening in Silver Benefit." It was pretty boring. Not the wealth of material I thought it would be. I would like to say that I just hung out in the bathroom and bonded with the men's room attendant, an old black guy named Alistair, but that was too depressing to do. Plus it smelled a little like poo-poo and pee-pee in there. I met two reporters for *Mother Jones* who put a book out about

the shadowy big businesses behind the push for ethanol development, but . . . why the fuck am I writing about all this? It was
boring. Fuck writers' parties. That's the last one of those I'll go to.
Let's get back to the good stuff—making fun of something Mary
J. Blige said!!!!

This is the front view of my family's summer home just outside of Atlanta. Inside we had an International Food Court—that's why we have all those different flags. We also had pretty good security for it too, since we got a lot of ding-dong ditchers, and my dad hated that.

This is a picture of me at the World of Coke Museum in Atlanta. Later that day I went to the Fruity Pebbles Institute and then the Memorial to Twittering.

This is from a sleepover party I had with some buddies of mine. I'm third from the left in the second row. "Hey Jason, lay off the Doritos, huh pal!"

This is from some porn I downloaded off of Ann Coulter's computer when I was at her house one day, cleaning the lint trap in her heart.

My fortieth birthday party, with a few close friends in Utah. If you look closely you can see my dog is crying.

The guy in the NASCAR outfit (C.C.) thought the guy with the dyed hair (Druse McLayney) was "weird" and didn't like him being out in public like that, so he paid him ten dollars to stand on his head in a pile of sugarglass.

This is from my sixth annual Hat Party. I came in sixth place and won two giant crab legs!

My girlfriend Cindee and I at the Center Center in Middletown, New York. We were there dedicating five pool chairs that we had raised money for back in Manhattan. It was a really fun day until that one asshole threw his daughter in the pool and she peed in it.

I spoke at this rally in Dayton, Ohio. We all tried to figure out what the answer was. We had a bit of a head start on the other rallies because we all knew that War wasn't the answer. We eventually settled on "Girl Scout Cookies, the mint ones."

I fucked around at my high-school graduation and had to do community service in order for them to release my transcripts so that I could get into college and get ripped off. I built this then.

This is super weird! If you look closely you can see the face of Jesus and the guy who played Mr. Drummond on *Diff'rent Strokes*!!! Seriously, look close. Closer, dammit!

Haha!!! I don't know who this is, but this dude is the funniest motherfucker EVER!! I was walking along Rue St. Denis in Montreal and saw this. OMG!!!! Hilarskis!!

I fucking HATE these two cunts!!!

Self-explanatory.

Grandmother Yehuda, Great-Uncle Barnabus, and me just before we went to see *Rent* on Broadway.

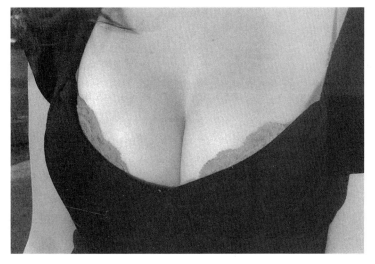

I took this photo of my then-girlfriend before I pushed her over a balcony in Cabo San Lucas on a dare.

Sweet Mary J.

RECENTLY, IN AN INTERVIEW WITH SOMEONE SOMEWHERE, THE lovely and unarguably talented singer Mary J. Blige said, out loud for people to hear, that "God wants me to have bling." Hmmmm, seems odd at first glance, but this may in fact be true. I certainly can't verify that God did or didn't talk to Mary, because I wasn't there at the time, but I'll go ahead and take her word for it—much like the rest of the planet takes the word of Abraham, Moses, Mohammed, Joan of Arc, Joseph Smith, Oral Roberts, Pat Robertson, George W. Bush, or that crazy lady in Houston who drowned her three kids in a bathtub a couple of years ago, who, like Mary J., were all spoken to by God while nobody else was around to verify it.

So we are left to take it on good faith that Mary J., if she's not lying, is correct that God truly does wish (or perhaps command) her to wear "bling."

Now it's not my place to say that Mary J. Blige is full of shit, although because I firmly and absolutely don't believe in God, much less one that whispers fashion advice, I can say, "I think she's full of shit," because I believe that God is a human construct and not real, and that it would therefore stand to reason that it is impossible for a God that I don't believe exists to do anything including but not limited to taking time from what one would imagine to be a very busy (I mean *packed*!) schedule to help a self-important American R&B star justify her narcissism and greed. But if you *do* believe in God, then why not believe that in the nanoseconds between shattering the left leg of a housewife from Taipei, making a rainbow in Gottenburg, Sweden, and allowing that guy in Oakland the strength and courage to rape that lady, all while simultaneously allowing a child of Christian Scientists in Santa Fe to die from untreated strep throat, that he chose to make his presence known to her (because that was the only time to get Mary J. alone that day, because she, too, has a busy schedule). And that God quickly expressed his desire that she wear bling just before scooting off to Yellow Knife, Canada, to make sure a grizzly bear decapitated an honor student before dawn.

Actually I should say "continue" to wear bling, as she had been wearing bling long before God ever chose to, seemingly unnecessarily, intervene. Sure, why not? God chose to make sure that Mary J. knew that he wished it that she adorn herself like so many Nubian princesses, with precious metals and gems. He talked to her about this, and only this, not about issues of morality or anything concerning spiritual guidance. He didn't even tell her where the treasure was buried! I guess he told her to wear bling in order to allay any guilt she might have had over such a selfish and vain use of precious resources. He did this so that she could feel better about herself. Basically so that she could feel better about herself for this simple blingish act as opposed to feeling better about herself and inflating her worth through an act of charity. Through helping others with a small stipend of the largesse, which has been given to her by millions of fans with neither her talent nor bank account.

Is there a correlation to be made between Mary J. Blige (whose God made his light known to her to assuage some guilt she might have had about the recent purchase of a 24-karat, white gold Rolex watch with kangaroo strap and sapphire centerpiece) and the semiliterate forty-two-year-old father of six who mechanically wants, hopes, and actually prays for some divine guidance to help him finally pick the winning lotto combination? You might think there is, but I say no.

I don't think so. Because one is lying, and the other is desperate for belief in at least one good thing in this permanently stained, unforgiving injustice that is life. The fact that Mary J. Blige is associated with a community that enthusiastically spends upward of 25 percent of their money* on useless (unless factoring respect-garnering or pussy-magnet abilities) vanity items like chrome spinning tire rims or diamond-studded platinum mouthpieces makes it almost questionable as to why she felt the need to proffer such a lame, unimaginative excuse for the ubiquitous ostentation that is commonly taught to be respected worldwide. Does it bring relief and peace to those working with international organizations trying to raise awareness of the brutality and absence of any respect for life that takes place in South African diamond mines, maybe even the mine partially owned by gospel-preaching and likewise wisdom of God's chit-chat recipient Reverend Pat Robertson? One would hope so. I like to imagine the latest rap artist making a video in which a giddily objectified, big-titted, big-assed whore of the moment undulates in a rubber skirt and six-inch stilettos while handing next year's "Where Are They Now?" award winner a silver plate holding different diamond fronts with his clever pun stage name embossed in rubies or emeralds or whatever other useless

*Totally made-up figure

and awkward foolishness he feels he needs to impress the afore-mentioned cock Dumpster.

I don't know if Mary J. Blige's God is the same as Billie Holiday's God or Marie Antoinette's God or Elie Weisel's God or Chief Sitting Bull's God or Stephen Biko's God. I don't know. I do know that it's not my God. My God likes those rope bracelet things that you get on Martha's Vineyard. I know that for a fact: He told me one time when I was sleepy and confused.

Hey! Free Advice!

It's been said several times by people smarter than me that I "know a couple of things about a couple of things." While some might read a cutting insult from this, I don't. Which makes me stupid and pigheaded. It is with this willful ignorance that I offer these unsolicited bits of advice to the world.

Dating Tips

There are as many opportunities on a first date to either blow her away with your wit, energy, thoughtfulness, and overall "awesomeittude"™ as there are opportunities to annoy, outrage, insult, and disgust that very same date. With that in mind, let me help you out with the following advice. And please remember, I get *major* puss! Seriously! Soooo many hot girls have let me put my thing in them and wiggle it around, it's nuts!

On your first date, refuse to tip even a penny. And make a big show of it. Then go into the kitchen and give the cook ten dollars. Then go to a bar and tip 300 percent on your bar tab. This will show that you are frugal and cost conscious. And that bartenders should be valued higher than people who memorize your dinner wishes and then bring you the food when it is ready.

What to Do if You Are Bitten by a Snake

Well, first, you should capture the snake alive. This can be done by making a series of gurgling sounds as if you are under-water* and luring it with a plate of maple sugar candies. Once you've captured it, it is *extremely* important to keep it comfortable. You will need to negotiate with it later, and everything you can do to ensure its trust in you will be very valuable. Trust me, I've been through this before. Once, I was on top of the sphinx in Egypt re-creating that scene from *Jumper* with some frat brothers of mine and I was bitten by an Alexandria Hamiltonya, which are not only poisonous but extremely litigious. Two months to the day after being bitten, while sitting in an Imam in Turkey, I was served with a summons to appear in an Egyptian court. I was being sued by the snake for libel. Libel!!! I was swearing because of the pain, not *at* the fucking snake. And it's a snake, so calling it a "dangerous snake" is not an insult! I eventually settled out of court, but it cost me a ridiculous amount of money. I don't want to talk about it. Actually, because of the terms of the settlement, I can't. But if you are interested, meet me at Niagara on the corner of A and 7th next Tuesday night, and I'll tell you all about it.

How to Have Fun at a Renaissance Faire

First, you'll need plenty of water, at least four oranges, a pillow-case made from flannel, some red dye #5, itching powder, two Fris-bees, a pair of lightweight binoculars, a DVD from season four of *The A-Team*, a small mirror, a prism, and some acid. The ingest-ible, fun kind. Take the acid and leave all that other shit behind the

---

*See my best-selling paperback, *Make Your Voice Sound Like It's Underwater in Twenty-Nine Easy Steps!* pgs. 17–23 and pg. 109. Published by Penguin Books.

Port-O-Let over by the Giant Turkey Leg stand. Now walk around and make fun of people to their faces. If you need any of that other shit while you're coming down, it's over by the Port-O-Let by the Giant Turkey Leg stand, remember?

How to Babysit for Mormons

Mormons believe in some crazy shit; they were the Scientologists of their time. Now (just like Scientology will become by around 2100, if it survives that long), Mormonism is actually considered sort of legit just by its rugged and often brutal perseverance in the face of logic and honesty and people intolerant of dangerous culty nonsense. When a Mormon asks you to babysit for their child, it is nothing to fear, but you should rather see it as an opportunity to educate yourself to the various tenets and practices of this fascinating religion that is sweeping the planet. Did you know that there are a number (two) of people in the Senate who believe in Mormonism? It's true, so let's give it the respect it deserves. When first arriving at the Mormon house, bow down and kiss the ring finger of the father's left hand. Then, rise up and give the mother a "butterfly kiss" on her clit. This is a way of showing fealty to the couple and dispelling any fears they might have that you might tell their impressionable children about Joseph Smith's (pre-prophet) time spent in jail in NY state when he pled guilty to fraud.

How to Totally Get Laid!!

I don't want to reveal all my secrets, but I can tell you my go-to, absolutely fool-proof "Secret Weapon for Totally Getting Laid," which is 100 percent guaranteed. Here it is, ready? Save a child's life. Works every time. The only difficult part is that you need to prearrange this to the letter. And it has to be set up far enough in advance so that everything falls into line as if by happenstance (but you and I know differently!). The key to this is knowing where you'll be going on your date, the route, and the time all of this will occur. Long story short, have someone set an accelerated fire to an apartment building within a public housing complex (these are notoriously shoddy since they are built for poor people usually by contractors with suspect business dealings cutting corners wherever they can—they go up in seconds). Make sure to have the fire visible from the street you're driving along as you're showing your date the "rough streets of the unforgiving urban jungle" that you were able to claw your way out of. Make sure that she sees the fire first. Slow down and say something to the effect of, "Oh, man, that's terrible. I hope precious lives aren't trapped in there. Where's the fire department? This is ridiculous . . . call 911! I'm going in!" Pull over and run in and find the child that was rented especially for this occasion and preset behind the mailbox hut safely away from the fire. There should also be charcoal to smudge on your face and a matching outfit that has been pre-singed for you. Change into the outfit, rub yourself with the charcoal, and run out limping and wheezing while holding the kid. Throw the kid in the backseat. Rush to the hospital, tell your date to wait in the car, and take the kid to room 113. Thank the parents, give them their fifty dollars, and go back to the car with a relieved but still shocked look. Continue your date. Back at your place you should pour two big glasses of girly drinks (as long as it doesn't have Baileys in it). And if you're with a lady who spends her free time scrapbooking, then Seagram's Peach Fuzzy Navels are the way you want to go. Trust me on this. Anyway, when you take your first drink, start to cry uncontrollably. Keep muttering about how precious life is, "all" life. And how we really need to make the most of every moment we have on this earth because we never know when it will end. Also, find a way through your tears to mention how long it's been since you've had a really good, wet, sloppy blow job. You're in! One hundred percent guaranteed.

What to Wear to a Funeral

No Tevas! That's rule number 1. Black is considered to be the first color (or lack of) you should choose in your wardrobe. However, if you cannot find any black to wear and the funeral was given with short notice (sometimes a sudden death can come at a very inopportune time, such as between games 6 and 7 of the World Series and you need to get that shit blessed and buried in a hurry!), then wearing blackface is perfectly acceptable. Unless it's a funeral for Cornel West. That fucker has *zero* sense of humor. Try not to get any on your teeth, though. That can be misconstrued as being offensive. As a side note, if it is Eve Ensler's funeral, you can do her no greater tribute then arriving dressed as a giant vagina. Bleeding through a series of well-hidden tubes, if possible. Also, be stinky.

How to Have a Perfect Soundtrack for Your Perfect Day

Okay, it's the first really nice spring day after an exceptionally long, morose winter. It's a bright, warm Saturday morning; you wake up and look out the window. The streets are filled with joyful people. Nine thousand of the most beautiful women (or men—whatever) on earth are floating through your neighborhood. Everyone is smiling and chatting. There's an energy and excitement that's been missing for months. You grab a cup of coffee, brush your teeth, unlock your bike, and head outside—but not before grabbing this mix CD that I made just for you to be enjoyed on this specific day (because I know how everything is gonna go down, trust me).

Enjoy these first five songs as you're tooling around on your bike, singing along, looking at everybody, and enjoying life with a big, self-satisfied smile on your face.

"Revelation" by Jason Falkner

"Kissing the Lipless" by the Shins

"Good to Me" by Brendan Benson

"Velvet Roof" by Buffalo Tom

"Wonderboy" by Tenacious D

Hey, isn't that Juliet and Emily and Jesse and Leslie sitting in the park? It is! You all decide to go to that new bar on Ave. B that has the windows that completely open so it's like you're sitting outside. And you sit and have a few beers and watch everybody. The next five songs are to be played while having your first two pints.

"Parallel or Together" by Ted Leo and the Pharmacists

"Dance to the Music" by Sly and the Family Stone

"Let's Go!" by the Apples in Stereo

"Naked Eye" by Luscious Jackson

"Twiggy Twiggy Twiggy vs. James Bond" by Pizzicato Five

Now you've got a pretty good buzz going. Everything is great, and your blood is made of ecstasy and unicorns. Enjoy these next songs during your next three pints along with the chili cheese fries you order after the fourth pint when it occurs to you that you haven't eaten yet.

"Sabotage" by the Beastie Boys

"Pounding" by the Doves

"Fox on the Run" by Sweet

"What's Your Name?" by Lynyrd Skynyrd

"Waiting Room" by Fugazi

"Oh, my God! I fucking love those last three songs! They bring back a lot of memories. Fuck, I used to date this one girl who was a photographer and she did this photo collage of Vietnamese punk girls—this was right when Vietnam first went all capitalist—and she was in Vietnam for like a month and a half and she brought back all these super-cheap CDs of '70s and '80s music that she got for like a quarter each. Her name was Heather . . . man, she was cool. Wonder what she's doing now? I bet she works for an ambassador or something. What if she has diplomatic immunity? Oh, man."

Now you are starting to get visibly drunk, and both your appearance and speech becomes sloppy. Despite your best efforts, you are becoming maudlin and emotional. You rapidly vacillate between sappy nostalgic and bitter nostalgic. Your friends decide to take a break from drinking, which incenses you. You call up one of your drinking friends who you're positive will come down and meet you. While you wait for him and nurse your next few beers, listen to these songs and start overanalyzing them and, while you're at it, their importance in your life. Also, whatever happened to the photographer girl? She was fucking perfect. Why did you let her get away? Maybe you blew it, huh?

"I Just Wasn't Made for These Times" by the Beach Boys

"He's a Whore" by Cheap Trick

"Blister in the Sun" by the Violent Femmes

"Clubland" by Elvis Costello

"Jealousy" by Liz Phair

Now your friend comes by and you have a few more drinks. The day and the sunlight drift on and eventually up, up, and away. At some point you become curious about the time. You make a mental note that it's probably around midnight. You find out it's 7:45. You're shocked but oddly impressed with yourself at the same time. You suggest that you and your friend get tattoos. He of course thinks you're kidding. Then your friend tells you about how he's thinking (just thinking, that's all) about asking his girlfriend to marry him. You are outraged. You tell him he's making a terrible mistake. Eventually you stupidly say that everybody secretly hates her. You immediately regret it, but foolish drunken pride prevents you from apologizing. You end up getting in a fight, and you both start crying. And when an old lady tries to break it up and in the process falls down and hurts her arm you are both shamed. You are kicked out of the bar after the cops come.

You decide to go to that Vietnamese place near Chinatown and get some fishhead soup in honor of your old girlfriend that you are now convinced you should look up, call, and try to get back together with. After several stumbling minutes of trying to drunkenly negotiate your bike lock, you ride off into Chinatown with your scraped left knee dripping blood, which you love the idea of. You find the restaurant, sort of lock your bike, and head in and order the soup. It seems to take forever for it to come (actually only three minutes). You take a couple of bites and immediately throw up in your lap. You are so humiliated that you can only laugh, which you do in the strangest, most maniacal way you have ever heard. You are beginning to frighten yourself. You throw a wad of money ($17, which is too much by $14) on the table and run out with puke all over yourself. Your bike has been stolen. You look around wildly, yell to no one, and start walking back home.

Here are the songs to listen to on your long walk home:

"I Think It's Gonna Rain Today" by Dusty Springfield

"Everybody Hurts" by R.E.M.

"C'est Le Vent, Betty" from the *Bettie Blue* soundtrack

"Bastards of Young" by the Replacements

"Colors and the Kids" by Cat Power

Once home you will eventually find yourself dancing around naked to the entire album *Quadrophenia*. You pass out (still naked) in a chair in front of your computer. You will spend the next two days indoors with your phone unplugged. And there you have your perfect day. In fact, you should listen to the song "Perfect Day" by Lou Reed and really think about what he's saying. Then cut yourself.

This is reprinted from the Guardian *newspaper in London. It was something they thought of to promote a stand-up show I was doing at the Soho Theater at the time (about three years ago at this point). They thought having Dave interview me as opposed to some stuck-up Brit would be better for everyone involved. It's pretty funny, and Dave Eggers will receive ten cents every time this is read aloud on public transportation, so it's for a worthwhile cause as well.*

Correspondence with Dave Eggers

From: Dave Eggers
To: David Cross
Subject: RE: FW: You v. David Cross, maybe

Hello David,

It's me Dave Eggers (of the San Francisco Eggers), I came to your show in San Francisco and pestered you about your pants. Do you remember me? I was there with my wife Caitlyn (to whom you were very attentive) and our nephew Utley who is a big, big fan of yours. Anyhoo, I understand you are going to be in London for the month of August doing stand-up at the Soho Theater. I know this because I have been contacted by the *Guardian* UK (a left-wing rag) about doing an interview with you. Does this "float your boat"? Get back to me and I'll fill you in.

Thanks,

Dave

From: David Cross
To: Dave Eggers
Subject: RE: FW: You v. David Cross, maybe

Hey Dave,

Do I remember you? The owner of the club was freaking out and practically hyperventilating over you. He made everybody wait while he had his girlfriend go home and get his copy of "The Staggering Heart" for you to sign. How could I forget? Anyway, I'm up for whatever you want to do with this interview thing. How should we go about it? Do you just want to send me some questions through e-mail and I'll answer them accordingly? Should they be serious (stuff about John Majors involvement with the Carlyle Group, or MI6's "supposed" snuff film studio), or light (questions about my days in the Kibbutz, or what my favorite British comedies are)? Let me know,

David Cross

From: Dave Eggers
To: David Cross
Subject: RE: FW: You v. David Cross, maybe

Hi David,

I've been in Surinam (sp?) doing an article about the black market banana leaf trade. Fascinating and dangerous stuff to be sure. I spoke to Nona about your idea for an interview to be put through the babblefish engine and she has advised me against it. They would rather have a straight interview.

Here's a few starter questions:

–As a two-time Mr. Olympia, are you worried about staying fit in London? I'm not sure if they have gyms or weights or anything like that there. They do have tanning beds, though.

–I think I first became aware of your comedy when you did that national Fiends of Funny tour with Gallagher and Jimmie Walker. You did some great impressions, just dead-on, of E.T. and of Dana Carvey doing the Church Lady. That last one was my favorite, because I think impressions are so funny. I sit there and marvel at how much you, David Cross, can sound like someone else! (I'm laughing, or sort of quietly chuckling, just thinking about it.) To me, that is comedy. Will you still be doing zany impressions? And what about the bit where you dress up as a piece of feces with Nazi sympathies?

I'm off to Melbourne to judge a shark carving contest (this is for real—I'll explain later). E-mail me with some answers.

Looking forward to your reply,

Deggers

From: David Cross
To: Dave Eggers

Dave,

Well, it seems as if we have started. In answer to your rather imperti- nent question of "staying fit" (your words—not mine!) in London . . . one does not get to be literally crowned Mr. Olympia once let alone twice (in three years) without rigid self-discipline and a steely reserve. Fish and Chips at three in the morning after nine pints of warmish ale and three shots of tequila? Perhaps once or twice just to indulge in the local culture, but certainly no more than three or four times or five times. I'm not one to snub my nose at my hosts so, to be polite, I would submit to this kind of activity if necessary to maintain good relations. Other than that it would be my usual routine of up every morning at 5:15, vomit, drink three raw quail eggs, run around in a circle with weights taped to my chest for half an hour, and then back to bed until noon. If there are no weights in London then I will use appliances that are approximate in weight. Surely they have toasters there. Isn't "toast" an Old English word?

As for the Fiends of Funny tour (originally titled "The Friends of Funny" tour until a typo went undiscovered and the press had already gone out), that's pretty much where I cut my teeth. I was a young, brash upstart and learned some invaluable lessons at the feet of the mas- ters. Jimmie Walker taught me the importance of delusion, and when I needed it most, Gallagher lent me his portable generator for my "What if God Was a Chinese Woman" bit. I won't be reprising too much of the old material, although let's face it, people love to hear other people sound like even other people, so I may dip in to some classic impressions (Woody Allen as Pinochet in heaven!) because today's audiences demand it.

I have been asked by *The Independent* if I will be doing my world famous "What if Eddie Izzard Wore a Suit" bit that I performed for the Queen shortly before one of her many liposuction surgeries. The answer is "maybe." I am going to ignore your transparent attempt at baiting me with the question about the "Krystalnacht Poo" sketch that you know very well was co-written by me, yes, but performed solo by Ray Romano.

Anything else, or can I go now?

David

From: Dave Eggers
To: David Cross

Just a few more questions:

I think the readers of the *Guardian*—a well-informed bunch, left-leaning, and perhaps outright Marxist—would want to know why an openly right-wing comedian like yourself would inflict himself on SoHo. That bit you do when you sing, via satellite, a duet with John Ashcroft—isn't that song just an Americanized version of the German national anthem?—I'm not sure how that's gonna play in London. Also, do you still wear eyeliner?

From: Dave Cross
To: Dave Eggers

Hmm, while "preaching to the choir" can be satisfying for the ego, at the end of the day it feels empty and useless. I will always be able to whip up a quick show for the quarterly fund-raisers of "The Sharp and Merciless Sword of Christ" and other groups I support, but where's the challenge? My three-week run at the Allen Ginsberg Theater in Berkeley, CA, is a good example of that. I was booed incessantly from start to finish by an audience of radical, drug-addled hippies. No one listened to a word I said, and the theater refused to pay me. Success! As for the eyeliner bit, I've always found gimmicks helpful to distract from lame comedy bits about *Star Trek* and the like. But apparently there is a fella in England who not only wears eyeliner but a whole ladies' getup! Oh well, whatever helps sell that stuff, I guess. I am going to continue to dress like a heterosexual man and rely on my material to create an impression.

From: Dave Eggers
To: David Cross

   You've been on a few TV shows in the U.S., *Mr. Show with Bob and David* and *Arrested Development*, but both of them seem weighed down by your presence. Have you ever thought about quitting them so the shows could be better?

From: David Cross
To: Dave Eggers

   After I auditioned for the part of "David" in *Mr. Show with Bob and David*, I remember thinking that I had really blown it. They were looking for an edgy nerd and I had just come from the American Douchebag Awards on MTV so I was wearing my Prada suit and sunglasses. But they were able to see through the real me and see that I could in fact play a socially awkward nerd, and they gave me the part. But in answer to your question, I struggled with that very dilemma often. I sought guidance from Jim Belushi, who told me that it didn't matter at all if I was talented or right for the part or not, that the best thing to do was not only ignore my obvious lack of any discernible talent or charm but to embrace my loutishness. I will forever be in his debt.

From: Dave Eggers
To: David Cross

Or a more serious one:

You've ranted about how goofy American protesters can be. When the war in Iraq was being pre-protested, you were on some of the talk shows, and you were berating the left for bringing bongo drums and dressing as clowns and generally treating an anti-war protest as a sort of hippie-love-in-party. And you're one of the leading liberal voices that's critical of how silly the left sometimes looks. There were more protesters of that war than at any time since the civil rights era. Were they ignored—by the media, too—because they looked like hippie freaks?

From: David Cross
To: Dave Eggers

I'm not so sure that they were ignored rather than dismissed. They (at least 15 million worldwide) seemed to be regarded with a sense of tolerated obligation, that this is what you get when you live in a free society, sorry folks. A protest would be shown on the news and treated like it was a minor annoyance, like a bad storm or an outbreak of flu. And while there were plenty of "regular" folks from all over the world who trekked to wherever because they felt it was important for their voices to be heard, it was usually only the radical stereotypes who got shown on TV because of, not in spite of, their inane, childish hippie outfits. Dressing up (inexplicably) like a robot wearing a multicolored afro wig, standing on stilts, and yelling that Bush is a Nazi at scared and disgusted middle-aged tourists only causes to make the already severe polarization (not to mention the fierce anti-intellectualism) in this country even more irreversible. Way to go, you dumb fucks.

Involuntary Random Thoughts I've Had Not Always When I Was Pooing but Certainly Sometimes When I Was Pooing

MAN, IT MUST BE SO FRUSTRATING TO BE THE SMARTEST COW IN the slaughterhouse field, or be the smartest cow in history, for that matter. I'm assuming that cows, like people and dogs, have varying degrees of intelligence. So at some point there was a cow of superior advanced intelligence running around a slaughterhouse somewhere that had figured out what was going on. That death was imminent, and all their masters were not benevolent nurturers but rather evil murderers luring them to their deaths. But he couldn't communicate this to the other cows because all the other cows were of average cow intelligence—i.e., stupid. Maybe even the cow was smart enough to know that he was just a cow and would never be able to impart the sense of urgency needed to escape because cows are stupid. Must've been maddening. Also, I wonder if we'd be less prone to eating beef if the noise a cow makes sounded less like "moo" and more like "help." Probably not. They're delicious.

———

I wonder if God cries. Or gets sad, even. Or happy. Or elated. Does he ever have a good belly laugh? Does he sense contentment? Does he feel pride or remorse? Is he stoic? We know from the Old Testament that he experiences bloodthirsty, murderous rage and fierce pride. He imbued mankind with all of these emotions, but it's hard to imagine him feeling any of these. It's almost a little embarrassing to think of him feeling jealousy. Of course he's WAY more advanced and evolved than we are. So I guess the ultimate stage of humanity is when we don't laugh or cry or experience emotion at all. God gave us laughter as a constant reminder of what lesser-evolved beings humans are. Stupid humans!

Whoever owns clean air is going to be fucking crazy rich soon!

Déjà vu is just the lazy man's version of telling the future.

I don't understand pedophilia. I think that one of the most unromantic situations that I can possibly imagine is making love, or rather, trying to make love, to a four-year-old. You'd be all, like, "Your eyes shine with the light of a thousand sunsets." And they'd be all, like, "What?" There is *nothing* romantic about it! How could you possibly make that "romantic"? With a four-year-old? That's just sex!

There's much you can tell about a man by sifting through his poo. Such as whether he's the kind of man who lets people sift through his poo.

I've been thinking lately about having kids. Not because I think they're wonderful, or I'm so desperate to have at least one person on my side who loves me that I'm willing to try to create one. Nah, fuck that. I'm thinking about having a kid so that I can justify my embarrassing amount of video-game playing.

You know what kind of person must have it pretty rough? A lesbian rapist. It's physically pretty hard to do. I bet that doesn't happen too often.

Life can be so unfair—like, do you have any idea what's going on in Darfur? I saw something on YouTube about it and I decided to write a check to the Red Cross, and as I'm tearing the check out of the checkbook, I got this nasty paper cut. It stung like a motherfucker! And I'm serious here, but . . . why me? I'm trying to make a donation . . . to help out these starving orphans whose mothers were raped and slaughtered in front of them! What the F? And to make things even crueler, the paper cut was on my video-game finger. I couldn't play *Gears of War* for like three days, either.

I have an idea about how to fix the Jew problem. By that, I don't mean that Jews are really a problem. I mean that there are soooo many people on the planet that have a problem *with* them. Except for the Chinese, as far as I know. They don't seem to have a history of caring about them one way or the other. Anyway, here's what I propose: let's take all the Jews not in North America and put them on an island somewhere—wait, hear me out. A beautiful, tropical island. It wouldn't be too hard; there aren't that many Jews in the world. There's only like 13 million of them. And over 6 million of those live in North America, so roughly 7 million. I know, it seems like there's more of them, but there isn't. We can give the Jews a chain of islands to live on. Something in the South Pacific or the Galapagos Islands or somewhere like that. An island where they would like to be. A place that would make them say, "You know, I must say, this isn't so bad, with the crystal-clear blue water, and the fruits plucked straight from the trees and whatnot. It could be a little more shaded, yes. But all in all, it's quite nice." Now, here's the stipulation. They only get to live there for two years. In that time, if the lives and economies of every Arab and

Eastern European country haven't changed significantly for the better, then they get to go back to where they came from and never be bothered again for the rest of history. You can make fun of their hats, but that's it!

What's the deal with them, anyway? They seem so exotic to everyone. I wish there was somewhere to turn to for answers about these strange and mysterious creatures.

Ask a Rabbi!

I HAVE BEEN CALLED, ON MORE THAN ONE OCCASION, IN FACT MORE than sixty-seven, a "self-loathing Jew." This is as irritating as it is lazy. I don't loathe myself, nor do I "loathe" Jews. I just find both to be equally annoying. Jews are the only culture accused of this, of being a self-loathing "something." You never hear the term "self-loathing Lutheran" or "self-loathing Calvinist" or "self-loathing Seventh Day Adventist." It's a perfect example of how Jewish guilt works, too. As opposed to Catholic guilt, which is all about disappointing God and his overly sensitive crybaby son, Jewish guilt is about turning your back on, or denigrating, your tribe. "How dare you! After all we've been through! Your uncle died in Dachau, and you have the nerve to disrespect your family and friends by questioning God's desire for you to never eat shellfish!?!" And usually the invective is thrown around when one apologizes for observed illogical behavior or they simply choose to leave the fold. I don't appreciate the accusation that I hate myself, because it's simply not true. And, in my own experience, I've fallen into that great Möbius strip of logic arguing my point, much like when a person decides that you are an alcoholic and then uses your startled, bemused, and fervent denial of this as proof positive that you are in fact an alcoholic because alcoholics are in denial of the reality of their alcoholism, etc., etc.

And if I'm not being accused of being self-loathing, then "condescending" is usually hiding just around the corner. I have heard and read this accusation dozens of times. And to a degree I suppose I have to admit it. But really, how can I *not* come off as condescending? Simply put, I believe that what you believe in (if you believe in God/the Koran/the Bible/the Torah/that you're supposed to handle snakes and speak in tongues/that you need to be "audited" to become "clear"/that Joseph Smith was a prophet/ that God will be very upset with you if you mix dairy and meat/eat meat on a Friday/it's okay to murder your sister or wife or mother if she "dishonors" the family by being raped, etc., etc., etc., etc., etc.) is utter nonsense and you are being seriously suckered. You are living a lie that you will never be able to rewind. I'd say that's pretty condescending, although not deliberately, sure, agreed. I will argue, however, that it's not nearly as condescending as thinking that anyone who disagrees with you is not just wrong but evil, dirty, impure, a lesser human, and resigned to a life in hell tickling the Devil's balls while he ass-rapes you in a lake of fire for all eternity. I'm gonna put it out there that that's WAY more condescending than my outlook. Of the very many scientific "theories" that get Christians, Jews, and Muslims frothing with anger, one of my favorites is the one that posits that humans evolved from monkeys. The reason it makes me giggle like a schoolgirl in a 1930s film is not that they think the theory is utter shit but that they are actually insulted by the idea. Insulted?! Where's the insult? What does that mean to you? Does it make the current you less of a person? This long, slow process started hundreds of thousands of years ago. It's not like they are implying that your grandma was a monkey fucked by a drunken atheist who broke into a zoo and had a little, harmless monkey-fucking fun and then you were born to a filthy human/ape hybrid. I mean, just exactly where is the insult? A monkey is the smartest animal on the planet and, like humans, one of the few that will indiscriminately kill its own kind for no practical reason (e.g., for food or procreation), so why is this so hard to fathom?

Anyway, I've gotten off the subject that started this whole mishegas; Jews, me being a Jew, other Jews, and me being not a Jew really but an atheist. So with that in mind, I present the following, which is funnier in the "ha ha" way than what just preceded it.

ASK A RABBI!

The following is reprinted with permission from *Jews!* magazine.

Hello! Gut Yontif! My name is Rabbi Yahuda McSeigleman, and I am a board-certified rabbi. I am a fifth-degree belted rabbi and am recognized worldwide for my cinnamon-sugar chometz. I have studied the Torah (which is sort of a Jewish Koran) under the tutelage of Rabbi Shmuley Mochebittzen and "Swingin'" Dick Reynolds. I have been doing this column for almost seven years now, and I have been asked to compile a "best of," if you will.

As a brief introduction for those not familiar, "Ask a Rabbi" is a biweekly column that I have been writing for *Jews!* magazine wherein I hope to shed light on a very complex, aged, and spiritual culture. Many of the traditions and rites of the Jewish people are misunderstood or are not understood at all. It is my pleasure to answer any and all questions regarding these truly fascinating and extraordinary people. Here are some of the more frequently asked questions I've received over the years.

Dear Rabbi,

How come Jews, the ones with the black coats and hats and curls, have such a difficult time understanding the protocols for flying on a public airline?

Tanyan Sturtz, Akron, Ohio

Well, Tanyan, you're referring to the ultra-Orthodox Jews who practice a stricter, and therefore more honest and correct, form of Judaism. While it may seem "annoying" or "impolite" to disobey the increasingly frustrated pleas of the stewards and stewardesses and captains and, eventually, other passengers of the plane, it is perfectly in their right to behave this way. This is because Jews are not bound under the general rules of the Federal Aviation Administration. They were given a dispensation by the Supreme Rabbi and Official Potentate Supreme and may do as they see fit. Sometimes that includes standing in the aisles, walking around distributing homemade kosher foodstuffs to other Jews, and standing up and putting their Torahs in plastic wrap while the plane is ready to taxi away from the gate. Sometimes they will also pretend that they don't speak or understand English while holding up the flight for everybody. While this may appear "rude" to the layman, it is really within their rights as a holy, holy people. "Holier than thou" is actually appropriate to say.

Dear Rabbi,

According to the Mansfield Stereotype Study in '98, the Jewish people have supplanted Puerto Ricans as the loudest culture. How did this happen? They usually shuffle along mumbling quietly to themselves in ancient languages, and Puerto Ricans are loud as shit. They're always yelling to people even if they're just two feet in front of them. Even their bicycles have boom boxes built into them! What gives?

Gene Garber, New Hope, PA

Ah, yes. The Mansfield Stereotype Study. If I had a dollar for every time this study has been cited, I'd have enough money to start my own bartering school to teach Jews how to effectively haggle with shop owners to get lower prices on their wares! That's how many times this Stereotype Study has been cited!! Gene, the findings of this study were thoroughly debunked almost immediately after it came out. It had numerous mistakes, the most egregious one being the inclusion of "noise made while eating" into the final factored study, which pushed the Jews ahead. As you know, only reformed, and some conservative, Jews are allowed to eat whatever they want without fear of retribution. When Jews who keep kosher are included, the list of available "noisy" foods plummets. No ribs, crab legs, Arby's Beef 'n' Cheddars, shrimp cocktails, oysters, crispy bacon, moules et frites, cheesesteaks, etc., etc. When the sound made by eating is not taken into account, the Jews rank 16th on the list, just behind Canadians and just ahead of the Dutch.

Hello Rabbi,

I was wondering if you could settle a bet I have with my wife. She says that Orthodox Jews are required by their God to perpetuate the species within such a small gene pool that there is rampant inbreeding, and this is why most of them are unattractive with terrible eyesight and teeth, while I say it's simply *because* they are ugly that they are the only ones who will have each other. Help! A lobster dinner's riding on this! Thanks.

Biff Pocoroba,
Piedmont, North Carolina

Well, Biff, guess what? You're *both* right!! Ultra-Orthodox Jews have created an extremely insular society where there are arranged marriages between few choices, so people who share the same gene pool often procreate, resulting in genetic deficiencies such as the aforementioned poor eyesight and scoliosis. Where "unattractive" is subjective and in the eye of the beholder, it would be disingenuous of me to pretend that they are often, not always of course, but often physically repellent to "normal" people. Let us remember, the Jew is not a unicorn! He is not a mythical creature that is beautiful to look at but nonexistent. The Jew is a living, breathing human being at least half full of life! Let us celebrate that!

Dear Rabbi,

I have lived in New York City for the last seventeen years, and since I moved here I have seen and continue to see the same Winnebago RV driving around Manhattan with the phrase "Moshiach Is Coming Now!" painted in large, faded letters on the side of it. I know that the word *Moshiach* means "Messiah" in Hebrew, but I'm confused as to their definition of the word *now*. Can you explain?

Pasquel Perez,
New York City

Pasquel, I have been asked this question a number of times, and the answer has always surprised people. Simply put, these people don't know what the word *now* means.

Dear Rabbi,

I live in Los Angeles in a section heavily populated with Orthodox Jews. And it occurred to me the other day when it was particularly hot (it was 101 degrees—this is a desert, don't forget!) that the Chasidim are perhaps the people on this planet that are being hurt the most by global warming. Because wintertime is the only time those people don't look absolutely ridiculous! And now that's being taken away from them. As

I looked at them walking along in their seven layers of heavy woolen clothes and fur hats, I thought, "There but for the grace of God go I." What do you think of that? Ironic, huh?

> Mark Lemke, Los Angeles, CA

Mark Lemke? From Temple Baruch Ben Yisrael on Fairfax? That Mark Lemke?

Dear Rabbi,
   Uh . . . yes.

> Mark Lemke, Los Angeles, CA

Why did you write such a thing? This makes no sense to me.

Dear Rabbi,
   Well, look . . . the Talmud teaches us so many wond—

Stop it! I'm a Rabbi myself! I know when you're stalling and don't have a real answer.

Dear Rabbi,
   What? What stalling? I'm asking a legitimate question! If I were to—

> Mark Lemke, Los Angeles, CA

No, no. You are a reformed Jew, pushing a liberal, progressive agenda, and this is unacceptable! You are trying to interpret the strict word of the Torah and "update" G-d's word to make sense in your enlightened world! Didn't you read the preface to this piece!? Go to hell, infidel!!

A Short Request to Lame Friends

I'VE ALWAYS FELT THAT LIFE SHOULD BE MORE THAN JUST A SERIES of unfortunate mistakes based on stubborn, lazy ignorance resulting in niggling little minor tragedies of what "could have been" begat from choices not made. I think life should be for the living!! And by that I am not saying no to zombies. I just mean that those who actively search out knowledge and experience should get the limited supplies of life-saving drugs or the last bit of oxygen before those who don't. And when we're faced with a life-or-death situation and we are called upon to prove our worth, please spare me your lame-ass lone drug story that you tell every fucking time someone brings up their acid, mushroom, DMT or whatever anecdote. Yes, of course! We all know. You were "totally high" off that pot brownie that one time and you thought you were gonna die and you almost fainted when you realized that you forgot it was your great-aunt's birthday and you were all going to the Ponderosa to celebrate and you nearly lost your shit when you saw Regina Conkle there but luckily she didn't recognize you and you were so paranoid that you just *knew* that everyone who worked there totally knew you were high, blah, blah, blah. I appreciate that you've been high and "out of control" before . . . once, but you *do* realize that I've heard you trot out that same story at least forty times before. And that's just *me*!

You seem to have only one story for each vice applicable. There's that drug story of yours. Your "drunk" story when you went camping in senior year and drank so much hunch punch that you threw up while you were trying to make out with that girl from Spanish class and you passed out on a frog and killed it and your friends had you convinced that you were supposed to go on a road trip to Vegas and it was your idea. And your "crazy sex" story about when you met that "totally hot" hippie girl in Vancouver who said she was a witch (the good kind) and was on her way to go to clown college the next day and she dragged you into the walk-in cooler in the hotel kitchen, but then she wouldn't let you go down on her and then cried after you fucked her. Yep, heard it. Thanks . . .

I'm just asking you to be a little more judicious with your stories. At least mix up the range of emotions and excitement a little bit. Please don't *always* pause and look away from us at that one part in the story where you describe the feeling of complete and utter irrelevance with your place in this world as you stared through the train window leaving Barcelona and you thought about killing yourself and how you'd do it before you ultimately snapped out of it and made friends with the African woman sitting next to you and how you should really make an attempt to get in touch with her. That's all. Just please try not to do at least that.

> Thanks for you time and consideration,
> David

Things to Do When You Are Bored

I'M ALWAYS AMAZED AT MY OWN ABILITY TO GET BORED. IT SHOULD be almost impossible in this day and age. Jesus, even if I ended up living on a chunk of ice floating just off the Greenland coast I would have, at the very least, *memories* of thousands of TV shows and movies and video games etc., etc. And that's on top of my real-life memories that have nothing to do with stupid little stories. How lazy am I that I actually toss my game controller aside, step over a pile of candy-coated magazines, click off whatever hilarious website making a witty point about whatever celebrity is in trouble for flashing her beaten snatch today, and stand arms akimbo looking out my window to Avenue A and pout like Donald Trump, shouting "I'm bored!" to the beautiful heavens above? There's no excuse, young man (me)! Get out and make something happen! Put down your "graphic novel" and get out there and make your own fun! Seriously! Here are a few ideas to get you (me) going:

- Murder someone who deserves it. Try it. I bet it's *way* harder than you think. You can't leave a trace or you will be living in fear of every knock on the door, every phone ring or fax noise. Although, come to think of it, you probably would never be bored again. Maybe I'm starting off too advanced. Let's step it back a tad and rethink this. How about these ideas:

- When an employee at a store (the Gap, or anywhere where you are hounded as soon as you enter by someone seeking a commission as a supplement to their minimum wage) comes up to you from behind and asks you if you need any help, act completely startled. Jump a bit and say, "Oh! You scared me!" and laugh a little bit to yourself. But don't stop laughing. That's the key. Laugh for about a minute and a half, always looking to the employee for some assurance, and then, in as smooth a transition as possible, start crying. Cry softly for a minute and then fall to the floor and take a nap, crying yourself to "sleep." Then refuse to leave until someone brings you a glass of warm milk. Buy one sock. Immediately return it.

- If you are on a long flight, bring onboard one of those S & M black leather, one-piece masks with no eyeholes and just a zipper for the mouth. Wear it, and when someone inevitably complains, explain that it's your "sleep mask" and you would appreciate not being disturbed. Try to do this in an aisle seat and keep your head as far out into the aisle as possible. At some later point, order a glass of wine and drink it with the mask on through your zipper hole. Then, with the mask still on, complain about how the movie is not "family friendly" enough. Also fart and get frustrated at not being able to smell it.

- Wear an iPod or any mp3 player (or a CD Walkman is even better) with big, noticeable old-school headphones, but don't have anything playing. Walk into a shoe store (or again, any store where you are annoyingly followed all around the store by an employee) and slightly bop your head to the "music" and hum a little and then every once in a while sing something about "getting shoes" or "shoe store." When the employee starts to strategically align him- or herself so that they can ask you if you need any help, pretend you don't see them and try to get them to follow you through as much of the store as possible. But always be enjoying your "music." As the employee gets farther away (but still when in earshot) start singing a little louder and completing more verses. Pick up shoes, considering them, while singing "lazy mother-fuckers in the shoe store. Need to get my shoes, but I don't know what to do. Why can't I get no help? All I want to do is get a new pair of shoes." Etc., etc. Keep doing this until the employee, now confused, comes over and taps you on the shoulder. Make a big deal about being into your song and not noticing at first. When you do notice, turn your iPod "off," and take your headphones off as well. Smile and acknowledge them. When they ask if you'd like any help, just smile and say, "Oh no, I'm just killing time while my girlfriend is trying stuff on." Then, put your headphones and iPod back on and start singing even louder about how the "dumbass shoe store clerk don't know how to help me. All I want is these Rizzeeboks in a size ten and a half. Can I get some goddamn help here?"

• Make a sandwich at the store. This is inspired by the open-ing of a Joe Namath movie I saw when I was a kid, and I thought it was the coolest thing ever. The movie was called *C.C. Rider*, I think, and like most great movies of my gen-eration, it was based on a novelty song. This is something that I've actually done before, and again, it's ballsy with-out being dangerous to anybody and has a mild, yet satisfy-ing "fuck you, Mr. Corporate Suit and Tie!" quality that

I would hope even the most uptight supermarket manager would be able to objectively appreciate. The title says it all; it's pretty much self-explanatory. Just walk into the supermarket and head to the bread section. Grab a split roll, go over to the condiment section, squirt a little mayo or mustard or whatever you like (some people like capers—me, not so much), then head over to your lettuce and tomato bin/aisle place. If you want tomato, you'll have to grab a plastic knife from the cutlery aisle. Take what you need (but *need* what you take!!!) from there.

- When attending a Major League Baseball game at any park where they sing "YMCA" during the break where the grounds crew comes on and tidies up the playing surface (I know they do this in at least Yankee Stadium as well as Ted Turner Field), turn to the people in your section and, with a big smile, shout out about how this song celebrates anonymous gay sex. "That's what you're singing about right now! Do you know why it's 'fun to stay at a YMCA'? It's because gay men can anonymously engage in anal and oral sodomy! That's what makes it soooo fun!!" Then mention how you are going up to the men's room into the third stall from the left, the one with the smoothed hole at about cock level, and you will be masturbating if anyone would like to re-create a fun "YMCA" moment. But sternly point to a young boy and say, "Not him, though. He's too young."

- Next time (and every time) you are in a hotel/motel/Holiday Inn (say what?!), take the Bible and inscribe, "Best Wishes, [Your Name Here]." Then make notes randomly throughout the book, circling passages and writing things like, "WTF?! Is this for real? Bullshit!" etc.

The Golden Age of Cowardice

I SUPPOSE WHEN MY FUTURE CHILDREN (HAMISH, 8, AND Dartagnan, 4) put down their holo-bears long enough to spend some time with their G.O.D. (Good Old Dad) and get around to asking me their inevitable and predictable questions, like "Dad, when you were a kid like me, what was it like?" or "Dad, was water ever free?" or "Dad, what was a *polar* bear again?" I suppose that I will smile, trying not to belay my weak fondness for nostalgia, pick them up, gently place them on either knee, and say, "Kids, your father had the privilege of living in the greatest time of cowardice this country has ever known." I will then take them to the "End Justifies the Means" Monument in Washington, D.C., and show them the majesty of the hundreds of thousands of lumps of hard, carbonized charcoal which represent the lives lost in the "Global War on Terror Part II: The Reckoning"© rising skydomeward that form the statue. I will stand with them as they view its majesty and explain: "Kids, on 9/11® America was attacked. After a brief nap our president eventually addressed his nation and urged the citizens he was sworn to protect to go shopping. Which is how we came to have the extra double-wide freezer downstairs."

Anyway, as you know, that date, 9/11, became known as the "Day America Lost Its Innocence."™* But kids, some clouds will occasionally have a silver lining, and this cloud had the most glittery one, for although America did lose its innocence, it simultaneously gained its ignorance! And that's no small feat. Can you imagine how difficult it must have been? For the world's (then) only superpower to move decidedly backward in thought and deed in such a time of serious and tangible progression was almost inconceivable. It would take a volatile and complex combination of state-induced fear, willful ignorance on a mass scale, an awakening of base intolerance, and a lolling, passive handing over of the basic civil rights this country once prided itself on as what separated us from almost every other nation on earth, thus increasing one hundred-fold the power assigned to the very same authorities who didn't do their job of protecting us in the first place.

I would explain to young Shanice and Grillith† that for America to gain its ignorance in such a speedy and life-changing way, it would take nothing short of a revolutionary act. Because this country was formed with the specific and then-revolutionary concept of religious freedom, as well as the rejection of the kind of secretive autonomous authority we find ourselves under, account-

---

*Not to be confused with Shays Rebellion, the Triangle Shirtwaist Factory Fire, the Trail of Tears, the executions of Sacco and Vanzetti, the lynching of Leo Frank, the Mormon Slaughter at Mountain Meadows, the Civil War, the McCarthy Hearings, the Death of Emmett Till, the Vietnam War, the Assassination of Martin Luther King, the Assassination of Two Kennedys, Watergate, Iran Contra Gate, the Bombing of MOVE, the Union Carbide Disaster, Love Canal, the tragic and disheartening "Discovery" of a "Sex Tape" Featuring Paris Hilton Sucking Some Greasy Douchebag's Cock, or the several other times when America lost its innocence.

†In the future you can change your kids' names whenever you want for as long as you live.

able to no one but a couple of Saudis and the Federal Reserve. So you can see, dear Autumn and Scooter, why a one hundred and forty degree shift was such a surprise. America had been fiercely and proudly fought for, it was a country with ideals so just and right and based in unwavering absolutes of fairness and concern for all human beings regardless of race, sex, creed, or class. But, as you both know, on that fateful day, a revolutionary act *was* committed by a group of men from Saudi Arabia, who hated America for previously well-articulated reasons. Part of the problem too was that they believed in a different Book than we did. The Book they read was much different from the Book we read. Both Books are very, very old and are interpretations of old transcriptions of anecdotes that had been verbally passed through hundreds of generations over the years in languages either dead or foreign to us. For example, it seems strange that, according to one of the multitude of authors of the New Testament, that God would want us to eat cow poo, but it states clearly in Ezekiel 4:15, and I quote, "Lo I have given thee cow's dung for man's dung and thou shalt prepare thy bread therewith." So there you go.

I watched from my computer as this country, led by TV, proudly pulled itself up by its imaginary bootstraps, which if not imaginary would most likely be manufactured by outsourced labor in Sri Lanka, or China, or Honduras or anywhere else the great gift of child labor is. But don't get upset, little Warwick and Ginnifer, child labor is illegal in America. You have communist unions and crazy liberals to thank for that. We would never stoop to such an uncivilized and blatantly un-Christian ideal. Nor would we ever condone it. Ever. *Ever!* Anyway, kids, that's when we collectively made a concerted effort to decide to go ahead and lose our innocence. We knew how hard this would be. What I mean by this is we were obligated to become an angry country. Our past history shows that America has never been angry or alarmist unless it was absolutely warranted. We were forced out of an idyllic reverie and

made to see an ugly, brutal world that lay just beyond our beautiful, well-fed borders. How could people act so crudely? So insensitive and barbaric? And according to the prevailing winds, these
were just the French! The French had had the audacity to agree
with the rest of the world who disagreed with us. What happened
to simplicity? What happened to simple folk doing simple things
and thinking simply? All of a sudden we allowed ourselves to be
divided into two groups, those who were either against us or were
for us. The Red States vs. the Blue States. We proudly drew up
lines of battle. The Red States, being the fattest and most illiter-
ate,* steeped in a proud, hundreds-of-years-old tradition of intolerance and piety, which ensured their obesity and stubborn ignorance
for generations, found themselves in the position of having to defend
their leaders from questions of incompetence, lying, collusion, graft,
treason, and, even worse, being *too* Christian, from the Blue Staters,
a loud, ineffectual, humorless group of braying know-it-alls who
didn't know all that much actually, who were equally as ignorant,
albeit about different things than the Reds. The Blueys thought that
wearing a T-shirt featuring a pun about President Bush with a word

---

*This is a proven fact. You can make of this what you will, but the fact remains,
where there are the largest groupings of "Red State" ideals, there is where you will
find the largest groupings of morbidly (and selfishly) obese and poorly educated
people in the country. It's also where you will find the most Christians. Now, before
you get all upset that a gay Jew nigger communist from an elitist college town is
saying all this, please keep in mind that it's the truth. It really and truly is. You
can choose to ignore this absolute like so many proven scientific facts, but there
it is. Also, since we're talking about it, do you think that the "Blue" parts of the
Red States are thriving economically, culturally and progressively *because of* or
in spite of the acceptance and therefore prevalence of homosexuals, multi-ethnic
communities, and various other progressive minorities? I know what my educated
guess is. Hint: It's the correct one! But what good is it to sit around whining about
stuff I have no control over? I'm no self-important blogger! America is number one
not just when it comes to infant mortality rates in the industrialized world (okay,
number two, fine), but also when it comes to top ten lists! We have more top ten lists
per capita than any other country in history. At any given time in America, there are
over one thousand top ten lists published for your edification and pleasure.

that sounded like "fuck" but wasn't actually that word was a ter-rible, crude affront. Yes, it was truly a ridiculous time, I will tell sweet innocent Jovanda-Mae and Wee Willy Whistfield. And then, after I've laid them gently in their pro-biotic chamber pods, I will whisper into their tender ears the words of the late, great, Rodney King: "Can't we all just shut the fuck up?"

Top Ten Top Ten Lists List

Entertainment Weekly's List of the Ten Greatest *Seinfeld*s in Order of Irrelevance

Readers Digest's Top Ten Ways to Make Lunch More Christian Friendly

Spin magazine's Top Ten post-punk neo nu-metal T-Shirts, Blog Sites

Kyle Tarkentun's List of Why Travis Booker Sucks

Golf Digest's Ten Best Whites-Only Golf Courses

Sylvia Plath's Top Nine out of Ten Reasons to not Kill Herself

Jesus' Ten Best Wet Dreams as a Teenager (Romans 13:9)

Der Speigel's Top Ten German-produced Fetishistic Scat Films and Reasons They Lost Two World Wars

L. Ron Hubbard's Ten Reasons to Sue Logic and Science

Andrea Dworkin's Ten Reasons Why a Pickle Is Better than a Man (hint: they're comically sexual!!)

Bill O'Reilly Fantasy

I DON'T UNDERSTAND HOW *THE O'REILLY FACTOR* AND THE *Radio Factor* are still on the air. By that, I mean allowed to stay on the air. The amount of misinformation that's disseminated from the host, Bill O'Reilly, is so vast and consistent, that you wonder what it would take. What absolutely, 100 percent wrong "fact" that Bill O'Reilly cites that becomes the basis for a twenty-minute diatribe in which his audience is encouraged to take his outraged position will be the straw that breaks the camel's hypocritical back? It's hard to imagine, given the egregiousness of his many "errors." I can't really think of another job where one would be allowed so many mistakes or actual lies. (Outside of "Page Six," TMZ, various gossip sites, politicians, cereal manufacturers, lawyers, P.R. firms, government officials, pundits, infomercials, the tobacco companies, pharmaceuticals, Monsanto, real estate companies, Henry Kissinger—oh wait . . . I get it.)

In a perfect world, knowingly lying about something would be a punishable offense. But it's not. Unless you lie under oath à la Scooter Libby, you can glide through the whole process like a greased pig on a buttered Slip 'n' Slide, and even then you can be pardoned. Think about it: if a history teacher at any level of teaching in any school outside of Appalachia or an Indian reservation, public or private, were to teach the same amount of completely wrong information that Bill O'Reilly dispenses each day, he or she would be rightfully fired. Then they would never be allowed to teach in America again. That shit may fly in China or Azerbaijan, but America? No, thanks. We'd rather have the facts correct, please.

Right? Hmmmm, maybe not. Okay, let's approach this differently. What might happen if video footage of a news/opinion show host from, say, Russia or Venezuela using the exact same tactics that Bill O'Reilly uses when engaging someone he disagrees with started making the rounds on the Internet. It would be used as an example of the dangers of state-run media in an authoritarian government. We would watch it and be thankful we don't have that kind of thing over here. We learned our lesson with the circus sideshow that was Morton Downey Jr. and Wally George. So it is curious and frustrating that not only is Bill O'Reilly not in jail and/or dead by his own contrite hand, but that, worse, he is a millionaire a hundred times over. If he were to call himself a comedian, of course, he could get away with a few fact boners (as I like to call them) every once in a while. But he doesn't. He takes himself seriously. So . . .

Back in June of 2006, I had been asked to appear in studio on *The O'Reilly Factor* on FOX News. This was due to this very story that you are now reading. Appearing on his show was not a decision I made lightly, nor was it made alone. I had seen first-hand Bill O'Reilly's mendacious, insulting, and immature way that he would conduct a "discussion" with people he didn't agree with or even remotely like. His was well-known and documented habitually uncivil behavior, and I wondered if I wanted to put myself through that potentially frustrating and deflating experience. I consulted several people, including many past guests of Mr. O'Reilly, and, after getting their takes on their experiences as well as advice, often unsolicited and imparted with passionate urgency, I called the show back and accepted their invitation. I felt a heavy sense of duty. I was David Cross to his Goliath O'Reilly.

There were numerous rules that they insisted I adhere to before I was allowed on. And these weren't just wardrobe ideas or verbal rules for while on the set. These were written in triplicate by his lawyers and held within a seventeen-page waiver that I had to sign and have notarized in front of three witnesses. Among the numerous points of interest in the waiver:

- You are not to mention Mr. O'Reilly's smell. It's a genetic problem that he has had since he was a teen. The clinical name is Irritable Syndrome, and it causes the host body to reek as if it were rotting from within, which it is, spiritually.

- You are not to get within six inches from Mr. O'Reilly's fingers. If Mr. O'Reilly starts to waggle his fingers at you, it is solely up to you and you alone to get out of the way of their path. Neither Mr. O'Reilly nor FOX News are responsible for any damages occurred from poking, pointing, and/or waggling.

- You are to take the blue pill forty minutes before the interview. You will take it with eight to ten ounces of water. Both the water and pill will be provided for you, although the cup will not be. You may rent the cup for a onetime charge of two dollars. Should you lose the cup you will be charged a onetime fee of thirty-four dollars twice.

- If you happen to be on the show during the official one millionth time that Mr. O'Reilly mentions his "blue-collar roots," there will be a brief pause in the interview, which will be signaled by a wailing siren. Several balloons will drop from the ceiling, and the "No Spin" dancers will enter the set to the "No Spin Zone" song (by country and western superstar Dilbert Creek). There will be a one-minute and thirty-second celebration, and then it will be back to the interview. Your name will also be entered into the giant drum, making you eligible for the grand prize trip to Aruba.

• You are to read and sign that you understand the Krugman Rule, wherein you are to feign ignorance and/or indifference to Mr. O'Reilly's misinformation. You are encouraged to say your point and get out as much information as you are able to, but if Mr. O'Reilly corrects you and you know for a fact that he is wrong, you are to address this in writing *after* the show has taped! This is very important, and failing to heed this will result in a suspension of appearing on not only the show but the network itself.

Again, this was a partial list of rules. I got a record of some of the past guests from a "for pay" website link from FNC (FOX News Corp.) and got in touch with the ones I was able to.* I heard from Tom Duckett, a truck driver for "Aunt Grannies Old-Fashioned, Country Tyme Chemotherapy." Mr. Duckett had been asked to appear on the show to represent the transportation industry drivers who were then claiming to be under intense duress due to the passage of the Pharo/Haman bill, allowing increased workloads and decreased available time allotted to deliver said loads. Mr.

---

*Quite a few had left the country, either on their own volition or were deported. And others had either committed suicide or died in suspicious circumstances, including one older woman who was beaten, dismembered, and found stuffed into several green olives, which were served at a cocktail party thrown by Roger Ailes to celebrate his winning the Coney Island Hot Dog Eating Contest, wherein he ate an entire six-year-old Indonesian boy who was in the process of eating hot dogs, in the record-setting time of two minutes, forty-two seconds. Although it was technically a hot-dog eating contest, he was given special consideration due to his diet.

Duckett explained to me that he was under the impression that he would come on and talk to Mr. O'Reilly about general "working-class experiences" and how, through driving in the heartland, he was able to see the real Americans out there and how they live a proud and simple life, unlike the fake Americans who live in cities on the East or West Coast.

He was slated to appear alongside Blaire Harmon, an ex-lobbyist, current rapist who was now working to educate the public against the dangers of a bill before Congress that would legally reduce the number of hours an employee of any business would be allowed to drive a truck. Mr. Duckett would routinely be asked to drive up to 2,000 miles and back in a forty-eight-hour period. Mr. Duckett, who initially welcomed what he thought would be extra income, had lost his ability to operate a truck seconds after losing his left eye and the use of his jaw for five months after getting into an accident stemming from a hallucination of a family of deer trying to cross the highway after he had driven for thirty-two hours straight. What he thought were deer were in fact a Mexican family and just one deer. Although, to be fair, the Mexican family was acting "deerish." Mr. Duckett found himself blindsided by Bill O'Reilly when, after correcting Bill that Montana's speed limit of 75 miles per hour was not "an example of the Socialists trying to take over," Bill called him a liar and a pinhead and went to lengths to say that his head was not unlike a pin. "Idiot," "fraud," "dangerous," and "anti-American" were also said, along with "jerk nose," "baby brain," "goofy gus," and "shit-storm Stanley," as well as "poo feet," "Indian-giver extraordinaire," "the opposite of decent," and "a real dink," once Mr. Duckett's microphone was turned off and burned. Also, "dickbuttballs," "stinky noise maker," "worse than Tutankhamun" "gold digger," "fascist elitist," and "caramel-coated candy apple faggot wannabe."

I rode my bike up to the FOX studios on Sixth Avenue and, after going through security (ID check, background check, voting record, retinal scan, credit report, and optional anal probe), I was ushered through the lobby and through to the second security area (flight records checked, blood test, urinalysis, B. F. Skinner box placement, Pledge of Allegiance, and optional anal tuck and roll). A pleasant but rather formal young woman named Gretchen greeted me with a smile and a chocolate American Flag. She was very nice but walked super-quick, though, as if I had a steadycam strapped to me and we were shooting a scene from *Grey's Anatomy*. Also, she wore an earpiece and bulletproof Kevlar vest. I asked her what was up with all the security.

"Ever since 9/11, we've been on threat level Ultra Red . . . or at least trying to be." She slowed as we approached a thick, foreboding door with an animatronic likeness (at least I think it was a likeness) of Sean Hannity. Gretchen stood in front of it and said, "You're a great American, Sean." "And you, too, my friend," said the robot, and the door opened. Everyone was really nice, and I was soon introduced to Bill O'Reilly.

He was more pleasant and avuncular than I expected, and as he graciously offered me a cup of coffee he told me how excited he was that I was on the show and mentioned twice how impressed he was with my courage for coming on. We talked very briefly about his newish book, *A Bold Fresh Piece of Humanity*. I asked him about the title and what made him decide upon one that could be so easily mocked. He told me he didn't know what I was talking about and asked what I meant. And I'll be honest here, I was more than a little nervous and hemmed and hawed. "Well, you know, you could substitute almost anything for the word *humanity*." "Hmmmm, you mean like 'cake' or something? *A Bold Fresh Piece of Cake*. Ha ha! I get it. That's a good one. I never thought of that." He said he had to get ready and thanked me again for coming on and walked into Hair and Makeup. While he got ready, I spent the next three hours reading the old copies of *Newsmax* and Alan Colmes's book *Huh?* that were prominently placed in my dressing room. Finally we were ready to tape the show.

I was the second guest on that night, following a panel consisting of William Bennett, Newt Gingrich, and the ghost of Dennis Miller discussing "What's wrong with kids today with all their rapping and drugs and video games?" I was introduced as the "iconoclastic author of *I Drink for a Reason*," and as I smiled somewhat tightly (I was still a little apprehensive about all of this) I felt a strange sensation on my ass, as if my chair had the tiniest mild shock going through it. I fidgeted a bit and tried to not let it bother me. I thought it might have something to do with my mic pack. After a couple of soft, friendly questions about how this book was doing, he asked me to share some amusing anecdotes about a promotional reading I gave at Brooke's Chinook Books, an independent book store in Fairbanks, Alaska, selling books to North American Indians and their salmon. I took the bait (no pun intended) and quickly got hooked by O'Reilly (no pun intended). He then began to reel me in (pun intended) and left me dangling on the line with a fishhook in my mouth (no pun intended) as I flopped around the deck gasping for air (no pun intended) like a fish out of water (pun intended).

As I started to mention giving a reading of a piece I had written entitled "In Anticipation of Reading This Right Now," which you'll find elsewhere in this book, he jumped on my general description of the salmon in attendance as being "one of the dumber fish out there." "Hey! Uh-uh! Not on my show, mister! That kind of invective may make your far-left zealot pinhead fans laugh, but it has no place on this show. NO PLACE!" It took me aback, and I stammered for a second, but then I got my bearings. I started to reply that it was just a joke, like my earlier joke about what if the holes in Jesus' hands and feet didn't heal up properly because of the lack of medicines available back then, and what he could then use the holes for when he got to Heaven in a practical sense. It was meant to be a lighthearted look at his Jesus, but O'Reilly refused to let me explain by cutting me off and going to the other guest.

I had a moment to think and calm myself down, and it was then that I again noticed the feeling in my seat like a mild shock, but it felt slightly stronger now. I tried to ignore it but couldn't. I debated whether to tell someone but ultimately decided against it. I didn't want to give the impression that I was nervous or, worse, crazy and just trying to deflect the charges. I started to interject and then the shock became unbearable. I lept up out of the chair and yelled involuntarily. As I did this, Bill jumped up as well (as if in anticipation) and grabbed my arm. While the other guest ducked, Bill pulled me toward him, saying, "Look, you little punk, you want to go a few rounds with me? Fine! You name the time and the place, and I will bury you, but I won't let you try to subvert my program!!" With that he pushed me back into my chair. The electrical charge shocked me once again and I jumped up immediately but this time made a sound that was closer to "owww" than the first sound, which was more like "nrgggh." O'Reilly ducked under his desk and then came up with a wooden table leg that he yanked off from the bottom of his desk. He lunged at me, swinging the table leg at my head. I managed to duck and grab onto the table leg with my left hand. I flipped over while still holding onto the leg and twisted his arm, dislocating his shoulder. I am hard-pressed to tell you what was more disturbing, the quiet crunch and pop sound from his shoulder or the girly scream of pain he shrieked out. He muttered some obscenities, saying, "Fuck it! We'll do it live!" before staggering to the back wall clutching his arm. Another guest was shooting the whole thing on his cell phone camera, which seemed odd as we were in the middle of taping. The floor director and producer came running over to me to see if I was all right. "I'm fine," I said, catching my breath. "Just a little shaken up. I'll be fine. Can I get some water and . . . holy shit! Look out!!"

O'Reilly had gotten back up and started running for the producer, a woman named Michelle. He was holding a razor-sharp copy of *Atlas Shrugged*, which he whipped at Michelle's neck. I checked Michelle against the wall and out of the way while hoisting myself up onto the desk and kicking the book right as it sailed overhead. It rose up and sliced a cable, which brought a 300-pound light crashing down. Bill, exhausted, slumped down and started to whimper. I walked over to him and knelt down. "Hey . . . what are you doing?" I asked. "What is this about?" Bill started sniffling, and his sobs became deeper and harder for him to control. "I don't know! I'm sorry. I'm sorry. I'm scared! I'm afraid I won't get into Heaven. I have sinned. Oh dear sweet Jesus, forgive me for all the pain I've caused. I don't know what's wrong with me." I patted him on his good shoulder. "Hey, it's all right. We all get like that from time to time."

"No. no, it's not all right. I'm a monster. A greedy, self-absorbed monster who doesn't know what the hell he's talking about half the time, and the other half, when I *do* know what I'm talking about, I'm lying through my teeth." Despite some misgivings, I gave him a hug. I gave Bill O'Reilly a hug. He thanked me and hugged me back. I could feel his hot tears soaking my sweater. "Okay, it's okay, let it out." He squeezed even harder. And then he slipped a hand down the back of my pants, which had become loosened during the ruckus. "Okay, none of that, now." He took his middle finger and slid it down the crack of my ass, which was slick with sweat. With one fluid motion he shoved it up to the second knuckle into my asshole. I jumped, which just made it worse.

"I love you," he whispered through sobs. I was very confused and also in a strange place comprising both pain and pleasure. "You need to take your finger out of my ass." He bit my earlobe and then said, "I've got a present for you." He stood up, with his finger still in my asshole, and haltingly, with his bad arm, undid his belt buckle. His pants dropped to the ground, revealing a pair of bloomers with a cartoon of a depressed duck sitting slumped over at a desk, saying, "I'm so happy I could just shit!" He wiggled his way out of the bloomers, revealing a gnarled but adorable penis, no bigger than half of a ladybug. Even from the ground five feet away I could smell what seemed to be a combination of raw sewage, scallions, and menthol. He waggled his tortured cock over my face and grinning said, "Don't worry . . . it gets slightly bigger." This was starting to get crazy. As I punched Bill O'Reilly in the nutsack and spat on his nub in disgust, the FOX security force finally got there. I was immediately relieved and gladly allowed them to force me up and handcuff me and drag me back to the green room where Neil Cavuto was getting audited by a pilled-up Greta Van Susteren. I can't say it was the greatest day of my life, but hey, how often do you get to punch Bill O'Reilly in the nuts? Even if only in a story, it's still very, very satisfying.

How to Play "Mafia," the Funnest Yet Most Unnerving Game Ever Invented

LISTEN, I LOVE GAMES JUST AS MUCH AS THE NEXT FELLA, BUT I, like you, tend to get a little apprehensive when one of my friends decides to hold "game night" at his or her (or *its*—not leaving you out, hermaphrodites!!) apartment. "Yay! We're gonna order pizza, y'all! And Brian is gonna bring his DVD of that duck getting shot by that kid on the lake!! You HAVE TO see it! It is BEYOND fucked up!!" If you are not logged into Evite, then please do so now.

Game nights usually start off a little slow and often a little awkward, then you kinda get into it for a bit, and then, once the beer has run out and talk turns to making a liquor store run, it peters out and you just want to take one more hit for the road and leave. Right? Of course I'm right! I'm talking to me! My personal favorites are Scattergories, Celebrity, Apples to Apples, shit like that. I guess because there's hyper, time-sensitive arguing that goes along with them. But . . . But . . .

But what if I told you there's a parlor game that blows those games away? This game makes those games feel about as exciting as attending a day-long seminar on something as mundane as how to paste photos into a scrapbook and what color crepe paper you should use to border said photos (by the way, the photo is of you and your family standing in front of Nebraska's largest potato salad). I, right here and now, am guaranteeing you a fun, emotional, exhaustingly good time. NO! Great time! Yes. Here it is:

And believe me, I know it sounds like the corniest Christian-camp-organized fun you could imagine, but seriously, please trust me; you will instantly become addicted to it, guaranteed. The game is called "Mafia," and a Russian psychologist developed it in the early '70s. Here's the deal: you get a minimum of twelve players (you can play with up to eighteen) and you sit in a circle. I know, I know, sitting in a circle is already pushing up the queer quotient, but bear with me. Everyone in the circle is part of the Village. One person acts as the "Mayor" who basically runs the show. I suggest making a male the Mayor as men are smarter at this kind of thing, and there's no danger of getting menstrual blood all over everything (*Ed. note*—a White male would be even better, no?). The Mayor then has the Village "go to sleep," which entails simply everyone closing their eyes and putting their heads down. The Mayor will then walk around the circle and, without making a sound, tap three people on the head. These people are now the "Mafia." The Mayor will ask the Mafia to QUIETLY open their eyes and acknowledge each other.* When this is done, the Mayor (again, it's important to have a man do this because a woman will start to silently think about everyone's shoes and get distracted) will have the Mafia close their eyes again and will then walk around the room, this time tapping one person, announcing "You are Detective #1." Then the Mayor will walk around some more and tap one last person, announcing, "You are Detective

---

*Now, it's extremely important that the Mafia do this quietly, because when the game starts there's usually some hyper pain in the ass who immediately starts saying shit about how "I heard movement over there! I heard breathing. I heard jewelry jingling! It's Brian! Brian's in the Mafia! He has a loose watch on!"

#2." The Detectives do not have to open their eyes. For reasons I will explain later, they do not want to reveal themselves.

Okay, now the hijinks begin. Basically the goal is simply this: the Village needs to kill off the Mafia before the Mafia kills off the Village. There are two rounds consisting of "day" and "night." At nighttime the Mayor (after announcing "It's nighttime; Village go to sleep") will have everyone close their eyes, then the Mayor (I can't stress how serious I am about making the mayor a guy, because at this point a woman will start to bitch about something she read in *Us Weekly* and take everyone out of the game) will have JUST the Mafia wake up and ask them to SILENTLY choose one member of the Village to kill. The Mafia quietly does this and, once the Mayor confirms the victim, close their eyes again. Now the Mayor will ask Detective #1 to wake up. The Detective is allowed to pick one person and ask the Mayor (again in silence) if he or she is in the Mafia. The Mayor either shakes or nods his head, tells the Detective to go back to sleep, and then awakens the other Detective. This action takes place each round until the Detectives are killed off.* More on this later, but right now it's time for the second stage—"Morning." The Mayor will now say, "Village, wake up; its morning," and everyone opens their eyes and lifts their head. Those new to the game that have been picked to be in the Mafia usually make a big show of "waking up"—it's a

---

*The cool thing about the Detectives is that no one knows who they are, and they kind of have to keep it that way. If a Mafia member suspects someone of being a Detective, then the Mafia will kill them, but the Detective does need to have enough sway so as to help the innocent or lay suspicion on the guilty. They have the hard evidence in hand. They have to try and subtly lead the Village to the truth. For instance, if they know that Jamaraqui (an awesome player) is innocent, but the Village, getting desperate, is singling him out to kill, the Detective has to somehow steer the focus elsewhere without being too obvious, lest the Mafia smell a rat and kill them in the next round. "I don't know. I gotta say, I'm not sure Jamaraqui is in the Mafia. He hasn't been farting, and usually he farts when he's nervous. But Toniqua, on the other hand . . . I think it might be Toniqua, because . . ."

pretty good sign of guilt, trust me. Now for the fun part. After a brief pause, the Mayor continues, "Village, wake up; it's morning . . . Brian, you're dead."

Oh, shit!! Now Brian (and all "dead" people) may not say a fucking word. They have to get up and out of the circle immediately without any of that, "Oh man I TOLD you it wasn't me! It's April! I'm telling you!" None of that. It is the Mayor's job to strictly enforce this rule, because some stupid people inadvertently give shit away as they're leaving. Brian will now stand outside of the circle and observe the mechanics of your friends lying to your face. This becomes, second to none, the best part of participating, once the game is moving along and the paranoia starts seeping into the room like so much Zyklon B. Now things start to kick in as the Village all talk amongst themselves, trying to suss out who's in the Mafia. Accusations are flung far and wide. Sometimes with some expertise and sometimes it's just a bunch of "I don't know, you just seem suspicious the way you're sitting there all un-suspicious-like" bullshit. The Mayor lets the Village prod and discuss for a few minutes and, then, based on the Mayor's discretion, will step back into the circle and call the Village to order.

Now it's time for people to make formal accusations as to whom they think is in the Mafia. If someone seconds someone's accusation, then the accusers explain why the accusation has been made. Then the accused is allowed to defend themselves. Usually there are two to four people accused per round. Then, when everyone is satisfied that they've had their say, a vote is taken. You only get to vote once each round, and you can't change your vote unless there is a revote. The person (let's call him Jaleel) with the most votes is killed. Again, they have to leave immediately and can't say ANYTHING! They can't do that half-mumbly "This is bullshit. I know Amy's in the Mafia, I'm tellin' you. You guys fucked up." The Mayor will then turn to the Village and say, "Jaleel was . . . [pause for nail-biting, hanging on the edge of your seat, dramatic effect . . .] NOT in the Mafia (or IS, if that's the case). Also, if Jaleel was a Detective (*Ed. note*—a BLACK Detective?!), the Mayor will note this as well. Now the shit starts to get weird. The Mayor should immediately have the Village go back to sleep. Sometimes you have to yell at the top of your lungs, "Village, it's nighttime! Go to sleep. Go to fucking sleep, for Christ's sake! Judy, this means you. Judy, shut the fuck up! Now, Mafia, open your eyes and choose somebody to kill." Well, this goes on and on until either the Mafia kills off the entire Village or the Village kills off the Mafia. As you can imagine, it gets really intense toward the end, especially if out of five or four players left, two or three Mafia remain among them. You get to see people pleading their innocence as if they were hostages. Husbands and wives will turn on each other and lie to each other's faces with an earnestness and stoicism worthy of Patrick Henry.

The real beauty of the game comes when you're playing your third or fourth consecutive game (each game lasts anywhere from half an hour to forty-five minutes, give or take) and you've had an opportunity from the sidelines to watch how slick or not so slick your friends who are secretly in the Mafia are.

Truly the best moment in the game (outside of being alive and on the winning team at the end) is, after you've been killed and have taken your place outside the circle, and your anger has subsided and you've gone to the kitchen with the other dead people milling about pleading your case, and you've guessed incorrectly as to who's in the Mafia and then the Mayor says, "It's nighttime, Village; go to sleep . . . Mafia, wake up and pick somebody to kill." And you watch as the people you weren't even close to guessing slowly and quietly raise their heads and pick off one more Villager. "I can't believe it's Tonya and Patrick and Leslie?! Those fucking assholes! Can you believe that line of shit she was feeding everybody about being too tired to be in the Mafia? FUCK! I can't wait to play again!"

I Don't Have Children

I DON'T HAVE CHILDREN, AT LEAST NONE THAT I KNOW ABOUT. HA ha! High-five me! (And by "know about" I mean that have survived.) But I imagine someday that I will. And I suppose that I will face the same difficult moral challenges that all parents face. And I suppose, too, that I will find those challenges, mistakenly, to be unique to my generation. What life lessons will I teach them? What lessons should be better left to television to teach? Where do I draw the line at individual freedoms? What little white lies will I tell about my past, and what dirty truths will I reveal? Should I leave the room when their generation's equivalent of *Keeping Up with the Kardashians* comes on TV? Or should I act as an addendum to the show and explain that if you want to attain a respectable level of celebrity in our culture, then there is no better, easier, faster way than to be videotaped sucking cock like a champ.

"Honey, I know you're only thirteen, and you're going through a lot of changes, and since your mom chose to leave us after learning how to drive, I have had to be both a mother and father to you. As well as a great-aunt, which I will explain when you're older, but come here, sit down. I wanna talk about something.

"Honey, I want you to know how proud of you I am, and how much I believe in you. And I know how much you're looking forward to going to American Idol Camp this year and learning to yell that one song from *Dreamgirls*, but if you really want to be a 'superstar' and live the American superstar dream of having people with low self-esteem and a marked lack of creativity wait on you hand and foot regardless of your treatment of them, eventually leading you to own a makeup line exclusively for puppies and angels, then you really need to abandon any kind of self-respect that I've hopefully instilled in you and get down to that silly Hollywood restaurant that Ashton Kutcher, Jeremy Piven, Sienna Miller, and the Church of Scientology own (it's called Prey, I think?) and get busy with the right people, if you know what I mean. Here, I want you to take this. This is a copy of *The Best of the Pseudo-Celebrity Sex Tapes, Vol. III*. Study it. Imitate it, and practice it. And sweetheart? Be mindful of the teeth."

Hopefully I'll be wealthy by the time my children are born, and they will turn out to be white and male, thus decreasing by 75 percent the "life's unfair" speeches I will have to give. But maybe they won't be. Maybe they will have a life that I could only gloomily daydream about (i.e., I, unlike my mother, would *not* raise them to be Jewish). Perhaps they will grow up to reject all things thoughtless and unjustified and find their way to my old punk albums and shitty mix tapes that I will strategically leave around the house for them to discover. Maybe at age fourteen they will want to put on a bunch of black eyeliner and go to some all-ages straight-edge punk shows at the rec. center. Will I stomp and stammer and have a 1950s/2005-era Christian Parent freak-out? Nope. I will excitedly point them in the direction of the club, help pay for their fake ID (they're not *all* all-ages shows), and gas up the car. Then I will wait at home for them and sit back proudly, knowing there will be at least one less asshole in the world. And with that comfortable blanket of parental satisfaction warming me in my den, I will secretly jerk off to the latest rackaliscious Jessica Simpson video. See! Everyone's a winner!

Good night, sweetheart.

A Short List of Videos with Babies in Them that I Have Not Seen on the Internet but Most Likely Exist and I Would Like to See at Some Point

A compilation of babies eating the poo of their household pets.

A compilation of babies being fed their pets' poo by the boyfriend of the mom of the baby.

A horse fucking a baby.

A baby throwing up in a stranger's mouth.

A boyfriend of the mom of a baby throwing up on it (the baby).

The incredible "no-armed, no-leg baby" (from Iraq).

A precocious baby, quoting H. L. Menken.

An entire greased-up baby being squirted out of a gay biker's asshole during a weird gay biker sex ritual. I guess the word *weird* isn't really necessary there.

A drunk baby trying to stand up and walk across the room.

A baby dancing to the cast recording of *Mamma Mia!*

A baby dressed up as G. G. Allin for Halloween swearing at people for candy.

Three babies balanced on top of each other.

A roomful of babies and one defanged tarantula.

A baby surfing and/or snowboarding with sunglasses that are too big for its face.

Two babies getting married for real.

A baby sitting in the toilet while rednecks laugh at it.

A baby duct-taped to a large dog that barks as the baby cries hysterically.

A baby tandem sky-diving.

A baby walking out of a public toilet stall who has been coached to say "Don't go in there!"

A baby who has been coached to say "Show me your tits!" during Mardis Gras.

Other Ways in Which Jews Can Utilize Current Technology to Get around God's Strict Laws for the Sabbath

PERHAPS NO CULTURE ON EARTH HAS MORE TO GAIN FROM THE advancement of robotic studies than Orthodox Jews. Due to an unwavering belief in unchangeable laws that were established thousands of years ago when people were, by today's standards, childishly ignorant, to put it generously, Orthodox Jews are handcuffed from living a normal life from sunup to sundown on the Sabbath, the most holy of days in the seven-day Gregorian calendar week. But the Jews are nothing if not savvy and have figured out numerous clever, conniving ways to get around Talmudic law, which is in part designed to show fealty and reverence to an almighty and at times petty, vindictive master. Some Jews figured out long ago that you could just pay the help (or a poor Palestinian neighbor) to switch on a light or cook your food for you. Some women even figured out how to look good on their wedding day, when your head is supposed to be covered, again, in a gesture to God, who presumably hates seeing hair grow out of a scalp. I'm sure God wouldn't arbitrarily create this law, which some of his creations might deem petty, or silly. The brides figured out that by wearing a wig made of human hair, they can cover their head with a virtually undetectable replica of their real hair and still technically they are showing reverence to God. Ha ha! Take that, God! Jews 1, God 0! What else you got, big guy? Gonna try to make me live in a dirty house because I can't clean it on the Sabbath? Fuck you! I'm presetting a Roomba. Didn't think about that, did ya, when you were making your list of egomaniacal, draconian "laws."

Forgot about man's ability to progress into the industrial, then technological, age, huh? You say I can't handle money on the Sabbath, but you didn't say nothing about training my dog to. I can attach things to my dog with Velcro and walk him on over to the bodega across the street. Don't test me, God. I got a million of 'em!

Beef with Jim Belushi

IT'S NO SECRET THAT I HAVE BEEF WITH JIM BELUSHI. AND I HAVE often used him over the years as my go-to utilitarian plug-in for any "lucky, marginally talented at best, annoying celebrity with douche bag tendencies" reference I needed in a comedy piece— whether appearing as himself in the semifictional, good-natured joshing of the Caldecott Award–winning "Cigar Corner" columns I've written or in a shout-out to his book, *Real Men Don't Apologize*, in my universally disliked animated program, *Freak Show*. Oh, and also there was the time I went to his ridiculous, self-indulgent "blues" show in Martha's Vineyard (that he had the audacity and outright shameless greed to charge forty fucking dollars for) and jumped up onstage a couple of times before getting thrown out of the club. You can see that on YouTube if you'd like. I'll explain more about that later.

But David, why Jim Belushi, exactly? "What did he ever do to you?" you may ask. There are soooo many undeserving douche-nozzles with inflated egos in Hollywood, why him? Why not Jeremy Piven, or Stephen Dorff, or whoever? Well, I've met both

Jeremy Piven and Stephen Dorff, and while Jeremy Piven was a bit of a dick to me, and Stephen Dorff wasn't a dick to me personally but rather to the valet guy outside of Mr. Chow's in Beverly Hills after a birthday dinner for Ben Stiller, neither episode really warranted a lifetime of sarcastic japery. And really, when haven't any one of us been a jerk to somebody before, whether intended or not? But my one, single experience with Jim Belushi was so noxious and unbelievably lowest-depths shitty that I feel justified for any cute, little, harmless piece-of-joshing fluff wherein I've mentioned him. And yes, there is an actual, real, honest-to-goodness incident that has driven my now very public scorn.

I've often been asked what the deal is, and time and time some more, I have patiently told the story. Sometimes at dinner or a bar, a couple of times onstage, but only when prompted—that's been my one rule. I never told the story unsolicited. Until now.

Now, for the first time, I will put it out there for all to read and judge. Maybe I'm being too harsh; maybe I'm not being harsh enough. Regardless, here is the story. And again, all true. Not an ounce of embellishment or exaggeration. Also, let me say this: if you think my opinion of Jim Belushi's work is undeserved, please get your hands on a copy of *Homer and Eddie* co-starring Whoopie Goldberg. It is one of the best/worst movies ever made, and Jim Belushi's performance is pure, unintentional comedy gold. Trust me, it's worth the hunt. Need a little teaser? Jim comically yet poignantly plays a grown man who's brain damaged and on his own. A modern-day Candide, with Whoopie as his street-savvy Dr. Pangloss. Just watch it. Oh! And even though his character was born and raised in a tiny rural town in Arizona that he's never left, he speaks in a thick Chicago accent. That must be one of those weird brain rewiring things that neurologist Oliver Sacks is always yammering on about.

Okay!! Here's the story.

In 1995 I was given my first real part in a movie. The movie was called *Destiny Turns on the Radio*, and it starred Dylan McDermott and Nancy Travis. As you might surmise, Jim Belushi was in it as well. Now, I not only had zero scenes with Jim Belushi, but I was never scheduled to even shoot within the same couple of days as him, so the fact that I saw him at all was a bit of a lark. I should preface this story by describing my very first time on set. On any set, really. I had driven out to the set during the beginning of the shoot to meet with the wardrobe department. I entered the trailer to find one woman softly crying (as if it was the end of a bigger, deeper sobbing session) and another woman alternately consoling her and cursing some unknown "him" who wasn't there. It was awkward and I kept my distance but made my presence known. I had never met these ladies before, let alone ever gone "to wardrobe." They gathered themselves and were very sweet and apologetic. I said something to the effect of "no worries" and then asked what was wrong. In brief, and I am paraphrasing from a meeting from thirteen years ago, Jim Belushi had come to set, hated the outfits that had been designed for his character (they were supposed to be cheesy and "lounge lizardish," as he was the underhanded, small-time manager of a floundering small-time casino), and took it out on the wardrobe women, berating them and demanding that they (against what had been written in the script) get him designer suits. Prada, Armani, shit like that. In other words, the opposite of what the character would wear. Now, I wasn't there for any of this, only the aftermath. And it was told to me by two women who were clearly still emotional about it. I couldn't be sure it all happened the way they described. But after meeting Jim Belushi, I had absolutely no problem believing it. Okay, moving on.

It is now the last week of shooting, and we are in Las Vegas at the Stardust Casino shooting interiors. As it happened, the scene I was shooting that night took place in the same location (the floor of the casino) as Jim's last scene of the whole film. As is much the case for every movie, I was called in much earlier than needed. I had already gone through "the works" (hair and makeup) and was in costume (a suit) and just waiting around with nothing to do but pick at craft services. I decided to play some blackjack while I was waiting for my scene to be up. I sat at a table across from where we were shooting but at a perfect vantage point to be able to see what was going on and when they would be finished and I'd be needed. Keep in mind that I had barely been on TV before so no one, certainly not this group of middle-aged and seniors from Oklahoma or wherever they were from, would ever recognize me, let alone assume I had some affiliation with the movie. I sat there playing silently, immensely enjoying everyone's speculations as to what the movie was about. The most ridiculous ideas based solely on watching, from afar where you couldn't hear anything, some people walking, then standing still for a moment talking, and then walking away. "I think it's about a guy who works at a casino. Jim Belushi's the star of it." Not quite.

Anyway, after about ten minutes of this, the dealer, a woman in her early thirties or so, says to the table, "I'm gonna try and get an autograph from him [Jim Belushi]. I have an eight-year-old son who's very sick and he's a huge Jim Belushi fan." Now, this is the one part you might have some legitimacy issues with. "What eight-year-old is a *huge* Jim Belushi fan?" you might say. But I swear to you that that is what she said. It was at this point that I spoke up and told her that I was working on the movie, and that I would get her the autograph. She told me her son's name was Michael and how grateful she was. "No problem." I cashed in, walked over, and stood to the side waiting for them to wrap the scene. After about ten minutes, "Cut! And that is a picture wrap for Jim Belushi!" The crew dutifully clapped as is the custom. I waited for this to die down, and as he started to walk away, I approached him. Once again, keep in mind, we've never met. "Excuse me, Mr. Belushi?"

"Yeah?"

"Do you see that woman over there?" I pointed across to the

table. "Well, she's got an eight-year-old son who's sick, and he's a huge fan of yours, and she was . . ."

Jim cut me off, curtly saying, "Jesus, I thought you were gonna get me a blow job."

The next three seconds are difficult to describe. I got very angry but tried to give him the benefit of the doubt, but no, there's no way he misunderstood me or I him. I could feel the blood in my face and my heart racing a bit. I took a big breath and then with a measured tone and overenunciation repeated myself. "No . . . she has a sick son who . . ." Jim cut me off again, this time angrier and even more dismissively with, "Jesus Christ, you're worse than my second wife," and walked away. I stood there. A little shocked, but that's perhaps not the best word to describe what I was feeling. Anger, incredulity, disgust. Those are better words. And I knew that I was going to have to go back over to the mom and tell her that I couldn't get the autograph. Who was more gracious than she should have been.

So there it is. A real, true-life tale of Hollywood assholeness. I still get riled up when I tell the story. I shake my head anew in disbelief at how vile he acted. I didn't see him again until the 2005 Emmys when he came out to present an award. I shouted "The Belush!!" as loud as I could, twice, hoping it would get picked up on air. It did not, but my friends nearby had a gentle yet cautious laugh.

So from this precious moment in time forward, enjoy some faithfully reproduced "Cigar Corner" columns culled from the back pages of *Cigars!* magazine with the edifying backstory in mind. Now, you'd have to be either retarded or the lawyer for this publisher to even ask if any of these are true, but in the spirit of being fair to retarded people who are reading this book, and/or lawyers, the following are not true. I repeat, none of these things really happened (that I am aware of). Anyway, here's the first one:

Cigar Corner

NEWSFLASH! "CIGAR CORNER" NAMED ONE OF THE TOP 100 CIGAR columns by *Cigar Column Weekly*!!

Hello, Pumpkin Pies! It's your humble cigar reporter, with the latest dispatch from the front lines of the cigar-smoking war, though it's not really a war.

Yours truly just got back from La La Land, and you're never gonna believe what happened. As you may or may not know, I am trying to secure the film rights to the video game *Madden 2002 Football*. I think it would make an excellent movie (I see John Goodman as the all-knowing voice of Madden), and since all the kids love movies based on video games, I figure this is like an idea made of gold and then covered in diamonds!

I met up with my agent, Ms. Delphine Santiso, an ex–child star from the View-Master series "Yellowstone Vacation" at that fun-time burger place ThumpWumpers. We were having dinner (when at ThumpWumpers, you simply must try the Onion Squealers!) when who walks in but . . . you guessed it . . . the Belush! "Oh shit!" I choked out. "It's the B-Dog hisself!"

I excused myself from my table, walked over to "Da Man," and pulled up a chair. I think he might have been embarrassed because he had just farted (I think), and that's probably why he told me to get the hell away from him, but I told him that I didn't care about his farting. He looked at me with that patented "I'm a miserable human being" look of his. "Uh-oh," I thought. "He's in one of his moods." That's when I produced from my portable humidor a Torquemada #4 and sparked that baby up for him. Well, that changed his tune. If there's anything the Belush can't resist, it's a cigar, or a passed-out babysitter! And since I didn't have the latter . . .

I started to tell him about how I want him to play the voice of Madden in my movie, and he stared at me like I had a couple of "Santiago Numbnuts" hanging out of my ears.

I reminded him of how he knows me, and just as he was about to grab the maître d' . . . Don Johnson walks in! He was with a teenage girl who, I guess, was his daughter, although she was Asian, but she kept calling him "Daddy," so who knows. Wow! The Belush *and* Don Johnson! If this is Heaven, then don't wake me up from my dream where this is Heaven!

After presenting Don with one of my prized Cuban Piffles, I asked if I could sit with them to discuss some "bidness." Don dismissed his daughter from the table and leaned in close.

"What is it, man? I'm hurting bad. I'll take anything."

The Belush started laughing at Don, and then the laughing became a wheeze, and then the wheeze became a little bloody, and some of it got in Don's good eye. So while Don went to the bathroom to wash up, Belulu took the opportunity to remind me that I had promised him the role of the voice of Madden.

"No problemo, mon amore," I said. "I was thinking Don could be the voice of 'The Guy Who Tells You That It's Halftime.' He'd be perfect!"

Beluminator thought about this for a second, and then a big grin crept onto his face. He pulled a hundred-dollar bill from his wallet, waved it in front of Don's daughter (who I later learned was named "Miss Saigon"), and said, "Well, looks like Daddy's been gone awhile. Maybe he doesn't know how to treat his little girl." Then the Belush accidentally dropped the hundred-dollar bill in Miss Saigon's lap. And I guess she was allergic to the money because when Belush went to get it back, she stiffened suddenly and gasped before looking down and softly weeping. I guess the Belushman felt bad for her allergies, even though he was smirking, because he then took her hand and pulled her up and away from the table and was nice enough to tell her about a job he had for her.

As they were walking out I yelled out to him that I would send him the information about the project. He couldn't hear me and just left. After the maître d' gave me the bill and informed me that Mr. Johnson had to go to the hospital for skin abrasions, I paid up and rejoined my agent at our table. I gave Ms. Santiso her diabetes shot and went into the kitchen to start washing dishes, as neither one of us had any money to pay for Mr. Belushi's meal.

"Oh well. C'est la vie," I said as I sucked on a "Clownish Brown" and scrubbed a saucepot. "C'est la vie."

Oldies but Goodies:
Delicious Chestnuts Dusted Off and Collected Here for Your Reading Pleasure

Some of these are things I posted on bobanddavid.com, and some are reprints from different magazines (and one very particular website). I am going to pretend that these have all been requested by different folks representing eleven different countries in three continents! Here you go.

Hudson News

LOGAN INT'L AIRPORT
300 TERMINAL C
EAST BOSTON, MA 02128

STORE: 00630   REG: 002   CASHIER: SEAN

I DRINK FOR A REASON
9780446697712   1 @ 13.99   13.99
SUBTOTAL   13.99
SALES TAX (6.25000%)   .88

TOTAL   14.87

AMOUNT TENDERED

Cash   15.00

TOTAL PAYMENT   15.00
CHANGE   .13
Transaction: 31956   1/2/2011 2:43 PM

Comments\Inquiries? (800) 326-7711
or Comments@Hudsongroup.com
Thank you for shopping with us.

0319560063000201022011

I DRINK FOR A REASON
9780446697712 -1 @ 13.99   13.99
SUBTOTAL   13.99
SALES TAX (6.25000X)   .88
TOTAL   14.87

AMOUNT TENDERED
Cash   15.00

TOTAL PAYMENT   15.00
CHANGE   .13
Transaction: 31956   1/2/2011 2:43 PM
Comments/Inquiries? (800) 326-7711
or Comments@Hudsongroup.com

Thank you for shopping with us

Hey everyone,

I was lucky enough to get my hands on an advance copy of James Frey's newest book. It's a soul-searching and no-holds-barred look at his life since appearing on the Oprah *show. This shit is crazy! What a tough life this guy has had.*

Excerpts from the Galley Copy of James Frey's Latest Memoir, *Lesson Learned*

From Chapter 1:

I left the Harpo studios in Chicago in a state of shock. When I accepted Oprah's invitation to go back on her show and tell my side of the story, I didn't think that I would be treated so unfairly. I felt as if a couple of angry skate punks who "didn't like my attitude" ambushed me. It reminded me of the time I was ambushed by a bunch of angry skate punks who "didn't like my attitude." I had awoken from a nineteen-day bender to find myself floating facedown in a canal in Amsterdam. I came to with a knife in my chest and a tattoo on my left nipple which mysteriously read: "100% Goth!!" I blurbled something in Arabic to a passing man on his bike, and he was decent enough to stop and fish me out. After drying myself off, I raped him and stole his bike. I regret this behavior now, of course. I knew it was wrong then, too, but that's what makes me such a monster. Or rather *made* me such a monster. That and all the drugs and alcohol I was addicted to. I'm better now, thanks to rehab. But that's an entirely different true story, which has already appeared in my last book, *An Unverifiable True Remembering.*

Anyway, after getting myself a breakfast (consisting of a fifth of Popovitch grain alcohol and some dirty socks I found in a garbage can), I set about looking for an explanation as to why I was in Amsterdam and where I could get my next "fix man." I lurched forward toward the Leidseplein to see if I could find Bruno Ganz, who always did right by me when I was in town. I made sure to catch all the projectile vomit I could into an empty Burger King bag that I carried around with me for that express purpose, for I knew I would be hungry later and would spend every coin I had on my "next fix." I had perfectly lurched no more than ten feet . . . or thirteen miles? Maybe it was thirteen miles. I can't remember exactly. This is a memoir, and that's French I believe for "memory," which, let's admit, is a little clouded by all the "drugs" and "alcohol" that I was totally addicted to. Anyway, I was walking along the plaza with my now useless leg. Wait, did I mention that I was so fucked up that I accidentally (?) let a transit bus run over my foot and didn't realize it until later that day when a young Amsterdamian child pointed to it and started to cry? Well, that did happen. I just remembered it just now, so . . . yeah.

Because of my now missing foot (I had it amputated without any anesthesia. I did this so that I could save $50, which I could then spend on getting a "fix" for my latest "high."), I was having a difficult time keeping my balance. Despite my best efforts I found myself bumping into a group of five gutter punks sitting on a curb. One of them got up and threw a kettle of boiling water in my face.

They were making tea, as I recall it. I said, "Hey now, what was that all about?" Which was difficult because the top layer of my face skin was peeling off. One of them mentioned not liking my attitude and I remember that setting off some crazy interior switch deep, deep inside me. Maybe it was because of my shitty worthless life or maybe it was all my self-loathing at not being able to make something out of myself despite graduating *summa cum laude* from the Sorbonne and almost being nominated for a Nobel Peace Prize for my work in the Congo, but when that switch switched it was as if my veins were drained of blood and filled with super-strong adrenalized Juicy Juice. I got an odd and calm look in my remaining face, stared the ten of them straight in the eyes, and said, "I'm bad, you motherfuckers. I'm a really bad man. I am so jacked up on alcohol and various speeds, like crystal meth, cocaine, ice, snowcaps, bobbyrocks, po-pos, jaggersticks, glass monkeys, and even two grams of pure Canadian sizzledots, that I can barely see straight. If you're not careful I just may eat your eyeballs with my rotting teeth (I had 'meth mouth' from all the alcohol I had been drinking). Now if you don't mind, I've got a date with a bottle of 100 proof Bukowski."

The twenty of them looked at me with the same curiosity that a Mexican ranch hand has when tending to the cattle, and he comes across a great big steaming pile of bullshit. They looked silently at each other and then back to me. After a tense couple of seconds the leader started to slowly but very deliberately clap his hands. One by one the others joined in and, picking up the tempo, parted themselves so that I may pass through. It was such a touching gesture filled with hope that it is seared into my memory, and I will certainly never forget it. I walked through with a newfound sense of humility and humanity. I walked for another couple of feet when I slowly stopped and turned around to express my grati-tude. However, much to my surprise, they had all vanished. As I looked about for them, I could have sworn I heard a tiny child's voice whisper to me: "You truly are the baddest mofo in all of the Netherlands. Go, and spread your word. But do it in book form. And not as fiction, either. Good luck, James Frey." And so that night I set down this tale on paper . . .

Chapter 2:

. . . Except the papers were confiscated at the border because it was determined that I was a security risk due to the fact that my vomit pants had blood on them. I had meant to wash either the vomit or the blood off the pants but had forgotten after I had gotten "high" by hyperventilating and spinning around as fast as I could after eating some heroin cake I had bought from an African. So I had to set about trying to piece the pieces of the story together. Honestly, there must have been at least a million pieces if not maybe a half dozen or so. I can't remember too well. I was so "high" on the fresh blood of the Burmese child that I drank in a "highish" haze that it's tough to get all the "facts" "straight." I'll do my best, though. That's all anyone can or should ask of me. Forever. Just to do my best.

Let's see, what happened? I talked about the one punky guy with the leather jacket throwing his cup of iced coffee at me and my face falling off and down on the dirty Amsterdam ground, right? (My face is deathly allergic to certain iced coffees getting on it—it stings!) I talked about how they jumped me and made me take out my appendix without any anesthesia. Man, what a mess I was. I desperately needed to get some help or I was gonna die. I wasn't about to spend my last days of life rotting in some prison in Ohio with a bunkmate named "Lefty" (serving six consecutive life sentences for raping and killing all of his cell mates. He was originally brought in on a misdemeanor for spray painting) and a ten-pound pet rat that I nicknamed "Aeolis" after the Greek God of the winds. No way, man.

I decided that rather than get help, I would break out of the prison that night or die trying. Much later in life I would decide to get rich or die tryin', but that's another (this) story. I set about looking for my way out of this hell that was the Ohio Maximum State Prison, officially* recognized as the most brutal prison in the world. I called over the guard who had stabbed me in the chin when I tried to beat him up for calling me a pussy the night before. He sauntered over and spit on me. I told him that he just made a grave mistake. I told him how one day I would write a book and mention all the wrongs I had been wronged, and everyone who ever crossed me would end up getting their shit called on in book form. Who knows? Maybe I would wind up going on the TV talk show circuit and telling the truth about the brutality that goes on in American prisons. I'm sure Montel Williams or maybe even Dr. Phil would be interested in my story. After that, he killed me.

More to Come Later.

Sincerely,
James Frey

*Prison Stuff Monthly.

A few years ago, after the release of my second humorous CD, It's Not Funny, *SubPop, the record label that put it out, sent me a request from the* San Francisco Weekly *to write something for them. "Sure, why not?" I said. "What do they want me to write about? My tour? The making of the CD? My take on the upcoming elections? This whole* Arrested Development *hoo-haa?" Well, no. None of that, as it turned out. The letter below is a great example of the predictable circuitousness of our particular form of propped-up, torn-down, disposable idea, and handling, of "fame." Anywhoozles, here's the request with my response.*

Original Message

From: Garrett Kamps
Sent: Friday, May 14, 2004 9:10 A.M.
To:
Subject: David Cross: Building My Backlash

Hey,

So here's what I think David should write: A piece about the on-the-horizon backlash against him. Last year there wasn't a hipster in the house who didn't want to give Cross a BJ for "telling it like it is." Now it seems those same hipsters are starting to tire of his sardonic 'tude. It strikes me that he's just about to cross over that line from hipster hero to resident asshole/punching bag (the TV show, "Eternal Sunshine . . .", and the *Rolling Stone/Spin* stuff don't help). According to the *Self-Loathing Hipster's Guide to the Universe*, David has two choices now: Go underground, provoke a string of rumors re: drugs, abortions, sweat shops; or embrace the backlash against him. I propose he do the latter in the form of a guest column in these pages. We could even get Eggers—no stranger to the backlash phenom—involved. Thoughts?

    g.

Hi. The above e-mail was sent to one of the guys in the SubPop publicity department to inquire about . . . well, you just read it, so you know what it's about. Apparently there will be some inevitable backlash against me, in part, because of the cumulative effects of the various projects I am working on. I suppose if I took on just a couple of these projects ("jobs" I like to call them, in my Protestant work ethic way) that might lessen some of the ill feelings that are slowly but surely working their way toward me and my sarcastic 'tude, but seven or eight of them in the same calendar year!? Forget it! That's got "Go away! I don't want to see your smirking face or hear your blah blah blahs for like two years, at least!" written all over it.

Here's my theory: Backlash and Backlash 2 are "inevitable" be-cause people feel like there is a somewhat vague sense of hypocrisy to what is now my life. I've spent years making fun of people and things both serious and light and have received growing attention because of that. Thus, I am now reaping the benefits associated—i.e., making money, getting on the guest lists of shows I want to go to, and fucking beautiful women that are WAY out of my league (and by that I mean my girlfriend, who is beautiful and WAY out of my league). That's part 1a. Part 1b is that the more work that I do that isn't *Mr. Show* or *Arrested Development* adds up to a whole bunch of stuff that, simply put, isn't *Mr. Show* or *Arrested Development*. Those shows were cancelled. They were great, and I'm happy to have been a part of HBO's pre-golden years as well as FOX's trash bin, but that's all over.

Now I earn my living by being a sarcastic crank, or "asshole," which is just one of my many onstage personas (I'm working on a new one where I amuse folks through gentle self-deprecating joshing, à la Garrison Keiller). I certainly understand why people would grow weary of my 'tude. I've felt the same way about others in my position. And I react with the same eye-rolling, "Yeah, yeah, whatever. You don't like the president and you don't like Hollywood douche bags, I GET it. Say, though, how was that bump that you did backstage at the White Stripes show in L.A.? I hope it didn't delay your guest VJ spot on MTV2 . . . jagoff" to others in my position. And this kind of thing compounds the problem. It seems that my career is entering the "Shut up already" phase. Those who were with me in the beginning before I showed my true colors as I willingly and exuberantly lapped at the feet of my indie heroes while preparing to play a game of televised poker with strangers are currently loading their blogs, ready to trash and deny. This means that I will now be left with just the people who recognize me from *Men in Black* or *Just Shoot Me* to look to for succor. I will while away the hours answering questions about what Will Smith is *really* like and whether Laura San Giacomo's breasts are really as big as they seem. Hmmm, actually that doesn't sound like much fun.

Okay then. With that in mind, I will turn to the aforementioned *Self-Loathing Hipster's Guide to the Universe* (published by Knopf) and plan the rest of my life accordingly. I can go underground (a real place; it is a cavernous lead-lined bunker in the Yucca Mountains in Nevada) with, amongst others, the guy from the Manic Preachers and Debra Winger. There I can bide my time and write occasional op-ed pieces for fanzines and websites under a fake name suggesting that David Cross is running guns in Columbia or hooked on opium in Karachi. All the while I will be scouring the Internet to see if sufficient time has passed to quell the backlash. Then and only then will I resurface in Iceland, years later, where I "had been the entire time." I will have a full beard, large pot belly, and a moderately successful eco-friendly bookbinding business that I will have run with my Icelandic wife, Gjo. I will make a brief appearance in the upper left corner box on *The New Hollywood Squares*, where I will renounce my American citizenship and show my new tattoo, then it's back to the bunker where . . . man, fuck that. I'm going to embrace my backlash . . . make it my own . . . cherish it and hold it aloft to the heavens like a newborn African babe. Yes. Bring it, I say. Let it inform me and shape me. Let the backlash give me new insight into the human spirit. Let it take me to greater heights and lower lows! Let it lift me onto a precipice from which I can see all! Let it change my outfits! May it swell to numbers too great to print in a family publication! If it means I get to work more, I'm all for it. See you backstage, fuckers!

Love,
David Cross

Okay, this is another thing that I wrote before I started writing this book that I wanted to include. I doubt too many people saw it when it first got posted. Do you know what pitchfork.com is? It's a website that basically reviews music but in a very, very precious and often overly verbose way. They clearly love what they do, but sometimes it can be a little . . . oh, sorry. I didn't realize you said you are already familiar with pitchfork.com. Sorry about that. I need to clean out the ol' ears, I guess. Anyway, here it is. And keep in mind that these are all real quotes from their reviews. I didn't make anything up or embellish at all.

Top Ten CDs to Listen to While Listening to Other CDs

Hi, I was somewhat surprised that pitchfork.com would ask me to participate in this. Here's why:

> The devastating paradox of David Cross's prerecorded comedy: Is it funny that everything Cross says is nauseatingly smug, yelped out in smarmy, supercilious prose? Or is David Cross just a giant fucking asshole?
>   That Cross is such an immensely unlikable live performer—condescending, defensive, arrogant, patronizing—is both his greatest asset and his most crippling flaw.

And while the above review of my second CD, *It's Not Funny,* is certainly more thoughtful than "David Cross? Yeah, he's funny" or "He sucks," it's still a bit shitty. "Immensely unlikable"? The paradox is "devastating"? How is it devastating?

And that's just one reviewer, Amanda Petrusich.* There's another one, William Bowers, who claims to:

> . . . having developed a strange, extra-textual concern for David Cross. Like-minded futon-psychoanalysts fret over his fluctuating weight, his fitfulness and despondence. . . .

Fretting over my weight? Oh, well. But regardless of their opinion of me and/or my act, they've asked me for my Top Ten List®. So here is my contribution to the Top Ten List® for pitchfork.com.

Top Ten CDs That I Just Made Up (and Accompanying Made-up Review Excerpts) to Listen to While Skimming through Some of the Overwrought Reviews on pitchfork.com

1. While reading over pitchfork.com's review for the Arcade Fire (here's a brief excerpt)—

> Our self-imposed solitude renders us politically and spiritually inert, but rather than take steps to heal our emotional

---

*One part of the Amanda Petrusich review I would like to respond to (and several people made this mistake; it wasn't just her) is the misinterpreted intent of the title of my second CD, "It's Not Funny," of which she said, "(oh, and the knee-jerk critical reaction to pre-emptive album titles? It's not funny)." It was meant to be a reflection of my feelings about the subject matter I was covering. Like when you're a kid and you're trying to tell people something that's important to you but no one is taking you seriously and everyone keeps laughing and your response might be, "Guys come on!! I'm serious! It's not funny!" So there's that, for the record. I could quibble about some other stuff, but just clearing the title issue is excitement enough for one day.

and existential wounds, we have chosen to revel in them. We consume the affected martyrdom of our purported idols and spit it back in mocking defiance.

—may I suggest listening to *Until It Happens/You Let It Happen,* by Maximum Minimum. The fourth album (not counting the re-release of the first three 7-inches on HugTown Records) reaffirms the band's status as the godfathers of the Taos, NM, "crying scene." Like a gilded phoenix rising from the toxic ashes of the death of mercurial lead guitarist, Peter Chernin, Maximum Minimum snarls back like a taunted tiger on steroids (also on acid). RATING—8.2

2. While reading the Pitchfork review of Daft Punk's *Human after All*—

Ideally, the physics of record reviewing are as elegant as actual physics, with each piece speaking to the essence of its subject as deliberately and as appropriately as a real-world force reacting to an action.

—(this is a real, albeit brief, excerpt) may I suggest listening to *Elegant Nuisance* by "ButterFat 100." With this, their second album since signing with Holive Records, ButterFat 100 return to their psychobilly/emo core roots. Let its volcanic rapture overwhelm you like a nineteenth-century hand-woven blanket made of human hair might have done back in the days when they enjoyed such things. RATING—5.5

3. While reading their review of Animal Collective's *Sung Tongs* (here's a brief excerpt)—

"The Softest Voice" layers clear-toned guitar figures upon each other, as Tare and Bear whisper in harmony above, as if singing to the vision peering back at them from the skin of a backwoods creek. The rustic, secretive manner of their voices and the barely disturbed forest around them suggests that whatever ghosts inhabit these woods are only too happy to oblige a lullaby or two. Likewise, the epic "Visiting Friends" gathers in faceless, mutated ghosts (i.e., oddly manipulated vocalizations from the duo) to hover over their dying fire in visage of nothing better than the tops of trees.

—why not listen to *As I Became We* by "Tishara Quailfeather." The virulent and hermetically sealed pinings of the world's only triple-gold-selling Native American artist living in an iron lung. It's as if newly dead, and thus still pure angels, reached down into the Virgin Mother's throat and gently lifted out the sweetest and most plaintive sounds man will ever hope to hear in this life. RATING—7.17

4. While reading the review of Blonde Redhead's *Misery Is a Butterfly* (here is but a brief passage)—

The word "lush" doesn't quite capture the fluttering whirls of strings, keyboards, and delicately plucked guitar that open "Elephant Woman"; I'd go so far as to label such enveloping richness of instrumentation "baroque," perhaps even "rococo."

—give a listen to *Turndown Service*, the forthcoming album by DotCom.com. Hopefully this foray into the electronic sector of the British no-fi/wi-hi scene (with apologies to Dr. Reverend Billy) is only a temporary diversion and not a full-fledged career move for Bix Xhu and friends. With a nod to early Creatures via the Monks, DotCom.com manages to wrench what little empathy one might have for the entire British working class (nothing you wouldn't find at an "Alive with Pleasure" show) and sashays it right up and down Trafalgar Square. RATING—6.22

5. While reading the review of the Boards of Canada's *Music Has the Right to Children*—

> The incredibly simple melody of the short "Bocuma" becomes a lump-in-the-throat meditation on man's place in the universe through subtle pitch shifts and just the right mist of reverb. The slow fade-in on "An Eagle in Your Mind" is the lonesome sound of a gentle wind brushing the surface of Mars moments after the last rocket back to Earth has lifted off.

—why not listen to *Only the Proletariat Flosses* by Screaming at the Mirror. With a truncated syncopation and approach that rivals only Tosh Guarrez pre-"FartFlap," S.A.T.M has taken steps to dismantle what was previously only dared mantled by the great Gilda Thrush when she fronted Cycle Clause. It's as if Genghis Khan got together for breakfast with Oliver Wendell Holmes and Virginia Wolf and ordered just a bowl of homemade granola and then skipped out on the check. RATING—11.–111

6. When you're enjoying the review of the M.I.A./Diplo album *Piracy Funds Terrorism, Vol. 1* (here's the beginning of that one)—

> Santa Claus, the Virgin Mary, and Terrence "Turkey-time" Terrence just got the shaft this holiday season. Why bother with presents? 2005's Tickle Me Elmo was supposed to be a chicken-legged Sri Lankan with so much sex in her self-spun neons you might as well get wasted off penicillin with Willie Nelson at a secret Rex the Dog show.

—(Huh?) check out University of Blunts' *Dirty Dirty Dirty Dirty Dirty Dirty*. It's like a 505 Groovebox as designed by someone who reads only Braille. Actually, to clarify, only if that same designer got caught in a transformer with Brindle Fly and decided to travel fifty years into the future and bring back what might have sounded retro thirty years from now if the future takes it's more than lugubrious, predictable course. RATING—4.001

7. Hey, are you reading the review to the Mountain Goats CD *The Sunset Tree*—

> As one would hope from a songwriter as smart as Darnielle, "The Sunset Tree" comes from a nineteenth-century religious song, "The Tyrolese Evening Hymn."

—why not have the latest Wittgenstein's Mistress CD playing in the background? On *Gift Code,* WM's latest offering, we find flutes aflutter, strings a stringin', and melotrones a melotronian. In what is likely to be remembered more for its chorus of "Get on the bed, bitch . . . now!" than its subtle and rich tapestry woven (most likely by candlelight) and suffused with an undercurrent of malaise and ennui, the titular track bends, breaks, and ultimately regenerates into a malevolent whirlstrom of angst and twee. RATING—Four Point Six and One Half

8. Trying to make sense of the review of Autechre's *Untitled?* It's a one-act play that starts with:

> *(Sitting in the dormitory room just after class on Thursday, Achilles changes into his gym clothes as his roommate Tortoise bursts through their door in a fit of happiness.)*
> *Tortoise:* Achilles, have you seen this?
> *Achilles:* What?

Tortoise: Do you see? Yes? I'm referring to the object, though small in size, quite interesting in stature, I am holding in front of you now.

Achilles: It's a CD.

And ends with:

Achilles: And my point is, if it's driven by form, it's a pretty messy, lazy form—certainly no more structurally sound than any other software wank music. On top of that, if I'm supposed to "feel" this, to pick up on some obscure metaphysical in-joke, I'm not—isn't it the job of a good artist to make that shit clear? Either way, it fails for me. Autechre decided to go their own way, fine, you know, just don't expect me to call them "geniuses."

Tortoise: [*Sigh*] Alright, Achilles, I can see we're going to have to agree to disagree. I'm sorry to have wasted your time.

Achilles: Oh don't worry, dude, just wear headphones when you play that stuff.

(With all apologies to Douglas Hofstadter and *Gödel, Escher, Bach: an Eternal Golden Braid*, which I'd send you if I had an extra copy.)

Why not give a listen to Pillow Logic's new disc, *Treason to Live*, a wiry concept album that gives new meaning to the phrase "Now, I've seen everything!" Ostensibly about a young girl who loses her shoes in a cockfight she mistakenly attends during Thanksgiving of '59, it's really about the universal themes of loss, angst, candy, and damp clothing. Taking its cue from the early commercial work of Deloite and Hughey and filtering it through the "I cut myself shaving" piousness of Throm Tillson, Pillow Logic reworks early sock hop chop flop and allows people like me to enjoy enjoying it. RATING—Two T-Shirts and a cup of jizz

9. Slogging through the review of Emperor X's *Central Hug/ Friendarmy/Fractaldunes (and the Dreams That Resulted)*—

> The aesthetic of Emperor X's recording belies its craft. Homemade and sometimes grungily recorded, the latest record by Chad Matheny's one-man band delivers jitter— and indie pop that practically gnaws its own arm with excitement.

—to try to find out if you might like it? Then don't listen to ThunderPussy, *When The Wild Birds Sing.* You can only shine a turd so many times before it gleams as bright as a six-year-old girl's ass cheek on Christmas morning. ThunderPussy answers the question, "How many times does one need to shine a turd before it gleams as bright as a six-year-old girl's ass cheek on Christmas morning?" The answer according to ThunderPussy is twelve. Twelve is the number of tracks on this CD, each one of the same song, "Star Wars!" And they all suck except for the last one, which shines just like a six-year-old girl's ass on Christmas morning. It's true. RATING—4.Point

10. Enjoying the self-referential Franz Ferdinand review, which includes the following?

> "Ryan, that cow is dried up. It's Gordita meat. I've even done the I'm-not-going-to-do-a-concept-review-anymore concept review," I said.
> "Hear me out. I'm seeing a comeback for one of your zany characters," Ryan said, making stupid TV-producer

gestures with his hands. "I'm seeing the interpretive dancer Santa Schultz, the Revolutionary War soldier Ham Grass, advice columnist Professor Rok, Diapers the glam-loving lab monkey, Justin Davies the bass player of The Hold My Coat, The Bummelgörk, Kelly the Masseuse, Volodrag the Yugoslavian sycophant, Paul Bunyan, Wolfie. Besides, you promised me the Franz Ferdinand review months ago."

Then don't listen to *Thar She Blows*, the terrible new CD by the Original Apple Dumpling Gang. If you like shitty, regurgitated slop as evinced by the over-lauded production team of Dr. Snagglepuss and Oppressor, then you're gonna love this. Daring to delve into his worn-out bag of used tricks, Dr. Snagglepuss turns to his old SugarSnaps partner, TreacherousFace ZombieHead, and spits out beats that sound like two dying frogs farting in your face. If that's your idea of an aural good time, then you're probably the kind of person that likes early Faust meets pre-post-op Neutron Bitch also meets Blunder (with a nod to Iceland's Achilles Healed) but then a fight breaks out and DNA Groove comes over and separates everybody and quickly escorts Neutron Bitch out through the service entrance, where they make love on a pile of day-old lettuce (like in the movies). Either way, T.A.D.G. do themselves a disservice by trying to milk some more milk from an AIDS-infested cow called "their old music." All in all, it's a big disappointment, but then again, if you like AIDS milk, then I guess this is for you. RATING—2.shit

Hi, everybody! The following is a letter I wrote after picking up Git-R-Done: The Larry the Cable Guy Story *(ghostwritten by Susan Sontag). I have to warn you that this letter is nearly nine pages long. But I think it's chock-full of life lessons for all of us, and if you're not careful, you just might learn something!*

An Open Letter to Larry the Cable Guy

HELLO, LARRY. IT'S ME, DAVID CROSS. RECENTLY I WAS SHOOTING something for my friends at *Wonder Showzen* (the funniest, most subversive comedy on American TV at the moment), and when we were taking a break one of the guys on the show asked me if I had seen some article in something somewhere wherein you were interviewed to promote your new book *Please-Git-R-Done* (published by Crown Books, $23.95 U.S.) and they asked about your devoting a chapter to slamming me and the "P.C. Left." Since I stopped following your career shortly after you stopped going onstage wearing a tool belt with cable wrapped around your neck (around your appearance at "Laffs 'n' Food" in Enid,

Oklahoma, Aug 23–26, 1999?), I said I wasn't aware of the article. They went on to tell me that you said basically (and I am not quoting but paraphrasing their recall) that I could kiss your ass, that I've never been to one of your shows (true), and that I didn't know your audience (untrue).

So, I went and got your book *Gitting-R-Donned* and excitedly skimmed past the joke about that one time you farted and something farty happened, on past the thing about the fat girl who farted, and finally found it—Chapter 5, Media Madness. Well, needless to say, I farted. I farted up a fartstorm right there in the Flyin' J Travel Center. I fartingly bought the book and took it home with an excitement I haven't experienced since I got Bertha Chudfarter's grandma drunk and she took her teeth out and blew me as I was finger banging her while wearing a Jesus sock puppet in the back of the boiler room at the Church of the Redeemer off I-20. (I don't care who you are, that's funny.)

Anyhoo, I got home and read the good parts. It seems that you were pissed off at *Rolling Stone* magazine, and I can understand why. You made some good points in your argument as well. I agree that there is an elitism and bias in the press, and too often a writer will include asides to show the readers how smart he or she is and how "above it" they are. But come on! Surely you can't be surprised, or worse, hurt or offended, by this. You even say in the book that you knew what you were getting into (*Rolling Stone* being all "lefty" and whatnot). Certainly I'm not surprised that they took a ten-minute phone conversation with me and chose to print only the most inflammatory paragraph within it. That's what they do.

But I want to address some of the things you write about me in *Git-to-Gittin'-R-Done*. In response to the *Rolling Stone* article, but first let me say this: you are very mistaken if you think that I don't know your audience. Hell, I could've been heckled by the parents of some of the very people that come see you now. I grew up in Roswell, Georgia (near the Funny Bone and not far from the Punch Line). The very first time I went onstage was at the Punch Line in Sandy Springs in 1982 when I was seventeen. I cut my teeth in the South, and my first road gigs ever were in Augusta, Charleston, Baton Rouge, and Louisville. I remember them very well, specifically because of the audience. I remember thinking (occasionally, not all the time) "what a bunch of dumb redneck, easily entertained, ignorant motherfuckers. I can't believe the stupid shit they think is funny."

So, yes, I do know your audience, and they suck. And they're simple. And please don't mistake this as coming from a place of bitterness because I didn't "make it" there or I'm not as successful as you, because that's not it at all. Since I was a kid I've always been a little oversensitive to the glorification and rewarding of dumb. The "salt of the earth, regular, everyday folk" (or lowest common denominator)—who see the world, and the people like me in it, as on some sort of secular mission to take away their flag lapels and plaster-of-paris Jesus television adornments—strike me as childishly paranoid.

But perhaps the funniest (oddest) thing in your book is you taking me to task for being P.C. Have you heard my act?! I'll match your un-P.C.ness any day of the week, my friend. I truly believe, and have said onstage amongst other things, that Orthodox Jews are, bar none, the most annoying people, as a group, that walk this earth. I absolutely refuse to say the term "African American." It's a ridiculous and ill-applied label that was accepted with a thoughtless rush just to make white people feel at ease and slightly noble. I also believe in the right setting that, as unfortunate as it may be, retarded people can be a near constant source of entertainment (fact!).

Larry, whether Northern, Southern, straight, gay, male, female, liberal, conservative, Christian, or Jew, I've walked them all. It didn't matter if it was a roomful of "enlightened" hippie lesbian

Wiccans at Catch a Rising Star in Cambridge, MA, or literally hundreds of students at the University of St. Louis (a Jesuit school), or a roomful of the cutest, angriest frat boys in Baton Rouge all threatening to beat me up, I un-P.C.'d the shit out of them. That's another thing that bothers me, too. I honestly believe that if we had worked a week together at whatever dumb-ass club in American Strip Mall #298347 in God's Country U.S.A. and hung out that week and got good and drunk after the shows, that you and I would've been making each other laugh (I imagine we would have politely disagreed on a few things). But not only would we be laughing, but we'd often be laughing at the expense of some of the audience members at that night's show, and you know it. I'll address your easy, bullshit sanctimonious "don't mess with my audience" crap further on. But for now, let's "Gittle-R-Ding-Dong-Done!"

Okay, here's what I said in the *RS* interview: "He's good at what he does. It's a lot of anti-gay, racist humor—which people like in America—all couched in 'I'm telling it like it is.' He's in the right place at the right time for that gee-shucks, proud-to-be-a-redneck, I'm-just-a-straight-shooter-multimillionaire-in-cutoff-flannel, selling-ringtones-act. That's where we are as a nation now. We're in a state of vague American values and anti-intellectual pride." You took umbrage at my calling a lot of your act anti-gay and racist and said that "according to Cross and the politically correct police, any white comedians who mention the word 'black' or say something humorous but faintly negative about any race are racists." Well, first of all, your act is racist. Maybe not all the time, but it certainly can be. Here, let me quote you back, word for word, some of your "faintly negative" humor, and I'll let people judge for themselves.

Re: Abu Ghraib Torture
"Let me ask some of these commie rag head carpet flying wicker basket on the head balancing scumbags something!"

Re: Having a Muslim cleric give the opening prayer at the Republican Convention

"What the hell is this the Cartoon Network? The Republicans had a Muslim give the opening prayer at there [*sic*] convention! What the hell's going on around here! Is Muslim now the official religion of the United States! . . . First these peckerheads (ironically, "peckerhead" was a derogatory word slaves and their offspring used to describe white people) fly planes into towers and now theys [*sic*] prayin' before conventions! People say not all of 'em did that, and I say who gives a rats fat ass! That's a fricken slap in the face to New York City by having some Muslim sum-bitch give the invocation at the Republican convention! This country pretty much bans the Christian religion (the religion of George Washington and John Wayne) virtually from anything public, and then they got us watchin' this Muslim BS!! Ya wanna pray to Allah, then drag yer flea-infested ass over to where they pray to Allah at!" End Quote. So . . . yeah. There you go. This quote goes on and on, but my favorite part is when you say toward the end, "now look, I love all people (except terrorist countries that want to kill us). . . ."

There are numerous examples, and I don't think I need to reprint any more. You get the idea. Oh, what the hell, here's one more: "They're dead, get over it! Poor little sandy asses! I'm sure all them dead folks they'd killed give 40 shekels or whatever kinda money these inbred sum bitches use, but I'd give 40 of 'em whatever it is to be humiliated instead of dead!"

About being anti-gay. I honestly take that back. I do not think that you are anti-gay; I didn't choose those words wisely. Your stuff isn't necessarily anti-gay but rather stupid and easy. "Madder than a queer with lockjaw on Valentines Day." That's not that funny, I don't care who you are. It's just sooo easy. I mean, over half the planet sucks dick so why gays? Why not truck stop whores, or Hollywood Starlets or housewives? Because when you say "queer" you get an easy laugh. End of story.

Okay, Larry the Cable Guy, I will ignore the irony of a big ole Southern redneck character actually using "inbred" as an insult, as well as the fact that a shekel is currency from Israel, the towel heads' sworn enemy. But at least you're passionate about what you see as inhumane injustice (not on a global level, of course, but on a national level) and the simple black and white of what's right and what's wrong. It's kinda like you're this guy who speaks for all these poor, unfortunate souls out there who wear shirts with blue collars on them, work hard all day to put food on the table for their family (unlike people who wear shirts with white collars or wear scrubs or T-shirts or dresses or costumes that consist of flannel shirts with the sleeves cut off and old trucker hats), and pray to the American Flag of Jesus to protect them from the evils of Muslims, queers, illegal immigrants, and the liberal Jews who run Hollywood and the media. I guess one could say that you're "telling it like it is." And considering the vast amount of oversimplification you employ to describe with sweeping generalizations all of America and the world that "don't make no sense to you," as well as your lack of sensitivity and second-grade grammar, one might be led to think that you are somewhat proud of not appearing (or being) too intellectual. Combine that with your sucker appeal to the knee-jerk white Christian patriot in us all who would much rather hear 87 fart jokes than hear a joke in which the president (the current one, not the last one), or the pope, or Born-Again Christians, or Lee Greenwood get called on their shit for being the hypocrites that they are, and I think we've got a winner!

As for being a multimillionaire in disguise, that's just merely a matter of personal taste for me. I do not begrudge you your money at all; it is sincerely hard earned, and you deserve whatever people want to give to you. What sticks in my craw about that stuff is the blatant and (again, personal taste) gross marketing and selling of this bullshit character to your beloved fans. Now look, if someone wants to pay top dollar to come to one of your shows and then drop a couple hundred more on "Git-R-Done" lighters and hats and T-shirts and windshield stickers and trailer hitches and beer koozies and fishing hats and shot glasses, etc., then good for you. I just think it's a little crass and belies the "good ole boy" blue collar thing you represent. But that's no big deal.

Now, as for the last statement that "We're in a state of vague American values and anti-intellectual pride." Well, I think that's true. When you can rally the troops (so to speak) with a lazy, "latte drinking, tofu eating" generalization of liberals and "black ass rag fags" to describe Arabs, then, yeah, I think that falls in the "ignorant" category. I think that with even the slightest attention to the double standard and hypocrisy of both the Left and the Right in this country (if not all of the Christian Extremists as a whole) coupled with the bullshit they lazily swallow and parrot back while happily ignoring the gross inhumane treatment of those that aren't them so that we may have cheap sneakers and oil and slightly less taxes (although I'm sure the bracket you're in now gives you a ton of tax money back), then you could maybe see my point.

Now here's the best part—in your book you preface the above quote by saying, "but I guess I'm not as intellectual as David Cross. In that *Rolling Stone* article, he sure showed us what a deep thinker he is by sayin' 'America is in a stage of vague intellectual pride.' " Jesus Christ, can you even fucking read?! Whoever read that article to you butchered the actual quote. The quote that was right fucking in front of their face! I would fire your official reader and have them replaced with a Hooters Girl who doesn't fart. That way you have something nice to look at while you are getting your misinformation.

As for "anti-intellectual pride," that is Larry the Cable Guy in spades. Let me quote you again (from an online interview): "I consider my jokes to be very jeuvinille [sic]. Stuff a fourteen-year-old would laugh at because that's the sence [sic] of humor I have."

Hmmm, okay. That was easy. Well, I suppose I've already covered part of that in the above. But you also specifically dumb down your speech while making hundreds of purposefully grammatical errors. How do I know this? It's on page 17 of your book, wherein you describe how you would "Larry" up your commentaries for radio.

What does it mean to "Larry" something up? Take a wild guess. The reason you feel the need to "Larry" something up? Because you are not that dumb. I mean you, Dan Whitney, the guy whose name the bank account is under. You were born and raised in Nebraska (hardly the South), went to private school, and moved to Florida when you were sixteen. This is when you developed your accent?! Not exactly the developmental years, are they? At age sixteen that's the kind of thing you have to make a concerted effort to adopt. Did you hire a voice coach? Or were you like one of those people who go to England for a week and come back sounding like an extra from *Lock, Stock and Two Smoking Barrels*? As you said yourself in an interview once, "I can pop in and out of it pretty much whenever I want." In your book on page 89 you say in reference to the "gee-shucks" millionaire comment, "see, to his [David's] mind, bein' well paid means I'm no longer real and I can't be a country boy anymore. It's just an act." Hey, it's always been an act!

That's my fucking point! You admit it yourself, so cut the indignation shit. And I am in no way deriding your work ethic. You clearly have more fart jokes than most, and for that I applaud you. You go on to talk about how hard you work and life on the road and living on Waffle House and blah, blah, blah. Yeah, I get it, we've all been there and played shitty, degrading gigs and sacrificed, etc., etc. Then you say, "This [the personal attack] was different because David basically hammered my fans in that *RS* article by implying that they were ignorant. He crossed the line when he railed against them, so I had to tell ya what I felt about that. He can hammer me all he wants, but when he screwed with my fans, it was time for me to say something."

Aww, that's so sweet and egregious. I can't stand that fan ass-kissing bullshit. You and Dane Cook ought to get together and have a "my-fans-are-the-greatest-people-on-earth-and-that's-why-I-do-this" off. You could both sell a shitload of merch, too. But having said that, I would truly love to get some of your fans and my fans in a room together to debate some of the finer points on comedy, music, culture, the issues facing our country today, and just about anything else we might find worthy of discussion. My fans are pretty smart as well. They are also, I imagine, as "hard-working" as your fans. Not all of them, of course, but most. And I'm sure that they may come up with some genuinely interesting, insightful points (and would do so without spouting a bunch of meaningless Christian platitudes). And if you really, truly want to respect your fans, lower your ticket price as well as the price of your ubiquitous merchandise. I'm sure all those hardworking Americans could use the extra money now that the budgets are being cut drastically from Transportation, Education, Health and Human Services, HUD, Dept. of the Interior, EPA, Farm Service Agency, FEMA, Agricultural, FDA, VA, FHA, National Center for Environmental Health, and numerous other departments and agencies that they might directly rely on for help. All so that we can pay off this massive tax cut during "war" time that we're all getting (them not so much, though). Oh, well. That's just one of those "political" things that I think about occasionally.

Anyway, I just wanted to address the stuff you wrote about me and clear some things up. Mostly the air around here . . . I just farted!!!!!

Think-of-Something-to-Do-and-See-That-Task-to-Completion!!!!!

Fart,
David Cross

We Have Got to Stop Calling
So Many People "Heroes"

PUT DOWN YOUR TUBE OF BED HEAD AND THINK ABOUT IT FOR just five seconds. How many people throughout history can you consider true "heroes"? One hundred? A thousand? Wrong. Science has proven that there have been literally millions of heroes throughout time and space. But of course the concept of what is heroic depends completely on the worshippers' values. To many, Martin Luther was a hero, as was Martin Luther King. But to others the guy who shot Martin Luther King was a hero. And then to even others the guy who shot *Martin Luther King—The Movie* or the guy who designed the Martin Luther King ride out at Six Flags Over a State are heroes. I could go on and on if my editors weren't such unfunny pricks. My point being that, one man's hero is another man's sworn and bitter enemy.

It was many a warm summer's night that found Mother and I listing gently on the veranda, leisurely sipping on gin and biscuits and debating who was the truer hero, a real retarded manboy or Cuba Gooding Jr. as "Radio," the fake retarded manboy. We never came to any satisfying answer, and we'll just have to wait and see what the Academy thinks come Oscar time. But the "hero" debate continues to rage across this vast and innocent land of ours, stretching into the sea and back. Will we ever lay down our arms and see eye to eye? No, not as long as there is some lonely, overweight woman down in the basement heading up the Accounts Receivable office blubbering on and on about how Laci Peterson is a true American hero. But we can at least agree to severely narrow down the criteria for being a hero.

Four categories have to be quickly and violently tossed out before we can go any further: rich and pretty and fuckers and athletes. Nobody should make it onto the hero list solely by virtue of the fact that they are rich. This means that anyone who has ever said or even thought to himself, "Dude, that guy who came up with the 'Girls Gone Wild' series is my hero. He's got his own helicopter and he gets to see drunk tits all the time!" cannot participate in this discussion that is not really a discussion.

Nor does being pretty make you a hero. What kind of pathetic loser thinks of a supermodel as qualifying for hero worship? Answer: either monumentally ugly people or other very attractive people, that's it. It is absolutely the least deserving of all the hero factors. Also people who manage to have sex do not deserve the mantle of hero. (Unless you live in a car and smell like the third day of the Burning Man festival yet still managed to fuck all of The Donnas, in which case you actually are a hero, and I raise a Coors Light to you.) And last, anybody who excels in sports. There is not now, nor will there ever be, a "hero of the gridiron." Nobody in his or her right mind should give a fuck about some well-padded millionaire with the reading level of a twelve-year-old home-schooled by Kip Winger, just because he tackled another well-padded millionaire.

So agreed, they are all out. Especially if you consider the billions of people who have quietly, with no expectations of earthly or heavenly glory, sacrificed their lives for others. Whether the sacrifice was literally their life or just a given life of leisure, these are the only people who should be considered heroes. I don't have any illusions that I will ever be even remotely like that kind of person. Selfishness, and a love of fine champagne and diamonds, combined with an ability to both ignore all the suffering that goes on around me and the talent to delude myself into thinking that when I do take some miniscule "action" that it actually makes some difference, ensure a life free of heroism. Jealous yet?

Yeah, it's time to retire the word *hero* outside of the aforementioned use. Let's save it for the truly self-sacrificing. Firemen? Heroes. Lenny Bruce? Not a hero. An important, groundbreaking cultural icon to be sure, but hero? Nope, too egotistical. Joan of Arc? Hero. Joan Jett? No. In fact, there is only one artist that can be considered a true hero, and that is Whoopie Goldberg. No, of course not. When thinking of Whoopie Goldberg as your hero, please, stop to think of criminally underappreciated Glenn Hoffstetler—that fucker ate seven (!) hits of acid and had forgotten that his parents were flying in that day from a long trip to Africa and he was supposed to go pick them up at San Francisco Airport. And he fucking did it! Now there's someone deserving of fame, fortune, and parades.

Oh, I Forgot You Could Do That

EVERY ONCE IN A WHILE YOU SEE OR EXPERIENCE SOMETHING THAT jolts you from your narcoleptic existence of useless pleasures and missed opportunities. And you are simultaneously reminded of both what can be and also of just how lame we are as a people, as a culture. Maybe it's an "art car," where someone has done something like nailed a couple hundred bloody Barbie heads all over it (I'm not saying that it has to be particularly clever, just interesting) or you see some lady wearing a dress made up entirely of "Have You Seen Me?" missing-kid things from the back of milk cartons. You see that, and you're reminded, "Oh . . . right, that's possible. " And I don't mean in an "Oh yeah, I guess there could be black Chinese people, I never thought of that" way. More like, "Oh, that's right, you can do that . . . I forgot."

And that is very telling about just how boring we are. It takes some fucking dipshit dressed in a beekeeper's outfit gluing used tampons all over his car to make us realize that *our* cars are boring. Ask yourself, "Why should I not paint my car? What's so great about maroon, and only maroon? What am I afraid will happen?

Will people not like me anymore? Will they think I'm some kind of lunatic? Will I be forcibly hospitalized? Will police arrest me? Will I never get laid again?" Well, I'll tell you what. Next time you see something like that, check out little kids' reactions to it. They fucking freak out. They start a contemplative journey that, if they're not excessively Christian and thus too far gone, can only end one way.

"My parents are lame and boring. They have absolutely no sense of visual adventure, much less any sense of any adventure at all. Good God, please don't let me end up like them, with their Mary Higgins Clark book reading, *Will and Grace* chuckling, 'Doctor Caruthers' Smart Popcorn Infused with Ginkgo Biloba' evenings. I know I'm only four years old, God, but if you save me from that life, I will fuck you forever when I get to Heaven, deal?"

We are always amused, from a distance, by the "eccentric" town characters that frequent our streets and provide us with a smile (though once they demonstrate the slightest desire to touch you, no matter how innocently intentioned, they're "disappeared"). The "Walking Lady," or the "Purple Man," or the "Retarded Child," or the "Post-It Note Guy." They are the ones who we see, and they delight us, while they also freak us out. Usually because we are not children. Because, as noted earlier, children dig them. It has yet to be drilled into kids' heads yet that this is *not* the way to behave/ dress yourself/make a living. So, not knowing that making a hat out of Post-it notes or making lampshades out of X-rays is ridiculous and wrong, kids naturally gravitate toward these things.

Here's a good example of what I am talking about: There is a musical act that I saw at the Bumbershoot Festival last year in Seattle (who have subsequently moved to New York City, where they are currently performing) called the Trachtenburg Family Slideshow Players. They are brilliant (in both the English and American usage of the word *brilliant*). They are nothing if not love itself. They are the embodiment of everything I just wrote about.

They are a father and a mother in their thirties and a daughter, about eight. They tour the country in their minivan (which is hand painted in many colors . . . why not?). They put on shows. They go to estate sales and buy the old slides of these various strangers and then write songs using the slides, in random order, as a guide. One of their songs is called "Mountain Trip to Japan, 1959," and that's exactly what the slides and lyrics represent. The father plays guitar or piano. The mom runs the slide projector. The daughter plays drums. Father and daughter sing the funny lyrics. And they kick ass. Jesus, the closest I ever got to something like that was when my sister and I turned off the lights, stuck candles under our chins, and read "The Tell-Tale Heart" to our humoring mom.

When I first saw them I felt something that reminded me of the feeling you have when you're like eleven or twelve and a not unattractive girl tells another girl to tell you that she might think you're cute. Blood rushes to your heart, and invisible ghosts keep turning your mouth up. And if an eight-year-old playing drums and chastising her dad in front of an audience doesn't make you smile, then something has gone terribly wrong in your life and you need to do one of those "Foxfire by Twilight" retreat-in-the-woods-type things with a bunch of aging, leathery hippies to find out what went wrong and help you get back on track.

"This is great!" I thought, but I hadn't yet figured out how to articulate what was great about it. It wasn't that it was "cute," or "funny," or "adorable," or "precious." It was what I've been talking about this entire time, you fucking moron. I was envious of that family. Now *that's* a way to raise a family and conduct your life that most of us either haven't thought of or simply lack the imagination and courage to carry out. They make every nutty home-schooling advocate look silly. And I'm not against the idea of home-schooling. I went to several (nine) different public schools up and down the East Coast and South, and the only things I remember from textbooks is that America is the greatest country the universe has ever seen and Abe Lincoln invented the tequila lollipop. I just get a little wary of most home-schooling advocates because they are more likely to engage in it not because of their lack of faith in public education but because, really, they're racists or religious nuts who don't want their precious little lambs exposed to reality.

Anyway, I'm getting off track. This mom, dad, and kid were getting into a crazy-painted van, driving cross-country, and doing shows about strangers' vacations? That's so much like the time my deadbeat dad pawned all of my shit so that he could afford to drive me back to Georgia from Arizona (where I went to live with him) because he had run out of people to scam money from and needed a new state's worth of suckers . . . oh wait, no it's not. I want her childhood. I want her mom and dad. I want to be eight and play drums with my family at nightclubs for hipsters who love me.

I hope when kids see them perform, that they have that same reaction as they do when they pass by the sculpture-strewn front yard of a house that has been altered to resemble a huge whale. You know, where they turn to their mom and dad and say, "Mom, Dad, look at that cool house!" and then when Mom and Dad, smiling, happily listening to Sting ("Something we can all agree on!") as their SUV drives past the house, turn to the kid and reply, "Wow, look at that." The kid will say, "Can we do that to our house?" And when Mom or Dad says, "No," that the kid will say, "Why not?" But this time, when neither parent comes up with a satisfactory explanation and ultimately resorts to the time tested "Because I said so, that's why," that the kid will turn to them and say, "Pull over. I'm out of here. If I want any kind of halfway decent shot at not living the rest of my life in mind-numbing boredom, I gotta take off now while the gettin's good. See ya later, losers!" Then, when that kid's older, I'll read his book.

For the Love of God!

I DON'T KNOW IF YOU'VE HEARD, BUT THE CATHOLIC PRIEST-hood just got a whole lot sexier! On February 21, the Reverend (Reverend—from Latin "reverendus," "to revere") John Geoghan was sentenced to nine to ten years in prison for fondling a ten-year-old boy. That might seem a bit harsh. Ten years for pulling down a kid's swim trunks and squeezing an underdeveloped penis? Hell, I've let worse happen to me for a candy bar. But I was in my thirties; this kid was ten and scared. Still, *ten* years?

But wait, there's more, as there most always is. Reading on you learn that this guy has over eighty civil lawsuits pending against him. One more time, in bold, **eighty**! More than 130 people have claimed various forms of molestation or **RAPE**. This guy must have thought he was invincible or something, maybe even divinely inspired. Perhaps protected by some like-minded force that would reward the good and punish the wicked. The wicked being non-believers or masturbators, of course. I don't know what else you thought I could've meant. Then you find that the charge of rape was thrown out because the statute of limitations had expired.

There's a statute of limitations on *rape*?! It's rape! It's not like you got ripped off by some online service and then you spent the next ten years thinking about whether you wanted to deal with all the hassle of reporting it and bringing it to trial. I would think rape would have a different set of rules. It is, perhaps aside from being tied up and forced to watch your children being eaten alive by your sworn enemy, one of the most life-altering acts of violence that can be perpetuated on another human being.

But maybe I'm overreacting. I suppose we should expect that any child, if raped, especially by an authority figure of unreproach, should act with the strength and moral outrage of an adult who, say, got overcharged for their dinner. They wouldn't take it, and neither should that kid. If at the age of seven he doesn't have the balls to make a formal charge, and it takes him fifteen years to get his "shit together," then fuck him. The rapist walks.

And now we come to learn that the church has covered up (that's right, actively engaged in a cover-up) and coddled and even helped relocate known pedophiles from parish to parish, all across the country, in cases too numerous to mention here. It truly is a "Brotherhood of Man," huh. They've even tried to pay the victims off. Nice.

But don't think that I'm trying to imply that it's just the Catholics who are at fault. There's a certain across-the-board kind of egotism that accompanies so many of those who are anointed God's very own spokesperson. This is for real; I know TWO different dominatrices who say that the majority of their clients were or are Orthodox rabbis. Beautiful!

It's certainly no secret that many priests are hypocrites and that one of their favorite ways of demonstrating this is by molesting little boys. And really, what better way to unwind after an angry, vitriolic denunciation of the evils of homosexuality then engaging in some man-on-boy frottage? And some people revile them as monsters, preying on the innocent and gullible (and I will not be dragged into that age-old polemic about how anyone who is religious should automatically be considered gullible—put a sock in it, Bertrand Russell!), using the powerful blackmail of entrance into Heaven as a way to cow the fearful. But I see them as humans. Humans who are the product of a confounding, medieval, intolerant religion based on superstitious nonsense and word-of-mouth that tolerates no dissent and is so proudly out of step with even the most basic tenets of modern, civilized thought that it all seems to resemble a game of *Magic: The Gathering* gone horribly awry.

I guess the lesson to be learned from the church is that while homosexuality is a sin against GOD, molestation and rape, well . . . they're just sins against a child.

Cigar Corner: Bonus Story!

By now, you may have seen the easily accessible afore-mentioned YouTube video of me jumping up onstage at a Jim Belushi and the Sacred Hearts "concert" (idrinkforareason.com/ Belushi!) he had the fucking audacity to charge forty bucks a ticket for (that's getting into Beck or Brooks and Dunn terri-tory!). This isn't about underscoring a very rich man's greed, unless of course he pays all the money to the band and doesn't take any for himself. Still . . . back in the summer of 2006, my then-girlfriend and I went to Martha's Vineyard for a couple of days to stay with some friends whose family had rented a house there for the summer. On the ferry heading over I was leafing through the local paper, the *Martha's Vineyard Tattler*, or what-ever it was called, to see what weekend activities there might be. I saw the ad for the show and got as excited as Bruce Vilanch at a convention for fat, hacky fags who wear "funny" T-shirts that your never-married great-aunt might find edgy. I ran up to my girlfriend and showed her my discovery. I was thrilled and I breathlessly told her that we all have to go and I should fuck with him. I think it was even her idea to videotape it. Eventually the night arrived and we all headed over to the Outerland, where almost two decades ago I did a mediocre comedy show (meaning I was mediocre) back when it was called Hot Tin Roof. If memory serves, nothing had changed much about this standard "road house" bar. Still, forty dollars to see a less-than-mediocre blues cover band consisting of mostly middle-aged white men living out some clichéd unimaginative fantasy as they plod their way through the millionth trotting out of "Sweet Home Chicago" should be considered a misdemeanor. If not legally, then at least morally. My girlfriend (let's call her Sarah) suggested that I wear a T-shirt reading simply "Worse than your 2nd wife," which is nothing short of brilliant. Anyway, you can see the results of that fun night of well-worn blues covers, the likes of which were virtually indistinguishable from the offerings of a band you might see at the Burbank Airport. Or playing in the lounge of the exact same shitty fourth-rate casino that Jim Belushi's character managed in *Destiny Turns on the Radio*. Delicious irony!!

Cigar Corner, Part 2

Hey, everybody, can you say "Holy smokes!"

Guess what, kiddos? I just got back from the Fifth Annual Great Cigar Smokeout on the White House lawn with the Pope of Cigars himself—Jim Belushi!!!! This yearly event is held to raise awareness, educate, and eventually legalize cigar smoking. Which is why you can bet donuts to dollars (dollars you can light on fire and then use the fire to light your cigar with—like the rich guy in Monopoly!!!) that if there's a cigar to be smoked, the Belush-Mobile will be pullin' up to the curb of Cigar Smoking and Jim Belushi will get out and smoke up a fatty! Which is exactly what happened!!

I was at Houlihans in the Georgetown area having some "Vertical Onion Rings" for lunch when all of a sudden there was this hullabaloo going on outside. I got the day manager from Staples, who was blocking my view, to move to the side, thus revealing one of the most glorious sights a CS (cigar smoker) could ever hope to see. It was—ready for this?—Jim Belushi!! He was getting his tip back from the valet when I spotted him in all of his Belush-filled splendor. I went outside to say, "Wassssssuuuupp!" (One of Jim's favorite "gags" is the Whasssuppp sketch from the Budweiser ads) and to see if Jim had any of the money he owed me from the crazy Hooters night in New Orleans. Jim saw me, and before I could even get out a "Whaaaa . . ." he grabbed me, put me in a big ole bear hug, lifted me up, and slammed me to the ground . . . ouch! He laughed, so then I started laughing, too. Man, that guy!!!

The Bubbaloosh lit up a Davenport Squish, took a few hits, and decided that we should go to see this friend of his named "Cheyenne Spread." She worked in a "gentlemen's dancing club." He said he had a surprise for her. I knew something wasn't kosher in Denmark by the way he spit on the ground and my shoes after he said the word *surprise*. My CS sense was telling me they weren't really friends after all.

We got in the Belush-Mobile (the same one from *K-9*!) and sped off. But first things first. I waited in the car while Belulu took a dump behind the parking lot of SaveTown. He borrowed my shirt to wipe his ass, and off we went to see Cheyenne. We got to the club, which, I have to say, gave off some strange vibes immediately. Right away they see Jim coming, and they make all nice with "Hello, Mr. Belushi" and "How's your current suite" and "We must insist that you leave a credit card this time," etc., etc. Enough with the ass kissing!! It's the Belush! He's just doing his thing. Which at this point was seeing one of his girlfriends. Jim lit up a beautiful Coco Havana Tanacana #6 and sucked away. I joined in the spirit by lighting up my own Rhapsody in Cigar (one of my faves!) and ordered a shrimp cocktail. After about a minute, "Cheyenne" came over and sat down.

Now, I don't consider myself the smartest chip in the cookie, but I ain't the dumbest, either. I figured out pretty quickly that this "girl" at our table had a bit of a secret, if you know what I mean; and what I mean is, that secret is that she's a he! In other words, a DUDE!!! I started trying to figure out a way to tell Jimbo without getting him upset or embarrassed. I needed to head this thing off at the pass before Jim got his horndog on.

I turned my head for maybe five seconds when they announced the latest dancer, "Big Man Tate," and when I looked back, Jim and Cheyenne were walking off to the VIP room hand in hand. Oh, man, I wish I could've seen the look on Jim's face when he felt around "down there" and instead of "tuna valley" he grabbed ahold of a dude's cock!!

I grinned like the Devil's nephew as I thought about that and lit up a Dunkirk Frightener.

After what seemed like an hour Jim and Cheyenne came strolling back looking like they were in love or something. I guess they just talked, because . . .

Oh, well. Leave it to the Belush!!!!

More later, kiddos,
David

Truck Stop

HEY, EVERYBODY. IT'S ME, DAVID, WITH MORE "SMOKIN' TALES" in the world of cigar smoking and smokers and also plain, old cigars that haven't been smoked yet, too, also.

Not much to report about this month. I'm heading out to Providence, Rhode Island, tomorrow for the fourth annual "Clowns, Cupcakes, and Cigars" bash, a family-friendly event benefiting "Cigar Smart," a worthwhile organization that raises money for impoverished children in poor, Third World, cigar-producing countries. All the money goes toward new shoes and finger skin for the little ones who work so hard rolling cigars so that we can unwind with a much-needed smoke at the end of our difficult days. Hats off to those kids down there; they work their tushies off!

Hold the phone! You're never going to believe it! It's tomorrow, and I've had a helluva day. I decided to rent a car and drive down to Providence. Driving allows me to catch up on my reading with my Books on Tape. Right now I'm in the middle of reading/listening to *The Pritikin Diet*, read by Gavin MacLeod. Anyway, I left at night so that I would have less Mexicans to deal with on the way.

About an hour into the drive I thought, "I could use some more Arctic Chill POWERade and Focus Nuggets." And, folks, let me tell you, those things *really* do work, by the by. It's definitely worth the extra dough for the fortified water. Treat yourself—it's your body, after all! Seriously, imagine that your body was a Christian temple. A temple that you'd want Jesus to get up into when he comes back. Well, you wouldn't build your temple out of simple bricks and wood and other junk like that, would you? Of course not. Not if you wanted Jesus to get up into it! He doesn't care to be insulted like that. You need gold and colorglass and precious marble. 'Cause when Jesus comes back he's gonna have a *lot* of temples (churches) to visit. And I'm sure the brick ones are gonna be way down on his list! Look, what I'm saying is, you should eat the food versions of gold and colorglass for *your* temple (church stomach).

Anyway, so I pulled over at the Lazy Cook truck stop just outside of Huntswallow. I got out of my car, stretched my legs, and pulled out a Dominican "Whistleblower." I had just started sucking on that baby when I heard a commotion over by the men's bathroom. I was a little apprehensive because I had a suitcase full of not-so-legal Cubano "Lil' Dictators" that I was intending to sell for the aforementioned charity. I stubbed out my cigar and fed it to a stray dog wandering around. As I quietly opened my car door, a truck-driverish man came bursting out of the bathroom in a panic. He was bleeding from his mouth and nose, and his "My wife's a fat pig, but I fuck her anyway" hat was askew. He ran right past me just as a lady came out of the same men's bathroom! Woah! I don't know what was going on in there, but this lady was pissed! She yelled out in this deep, guttural, manly voice: "Give me my money, asshole!" She lurched past me, but she didn't get two steps before her heel broke. She fell to her knees and skidded forward. She stayed there for a minute on all fours, staring at the ground. It was really awkward, and I wasn't sure what to do. Then it seemed like she was laughing. "Heh, heh. I guess he didn't know that it was occupied, huh?" That's what I said. She just kept looking at the ground. Then she grabbed the bumper of my car and started to lift herself up, but then she just collapsed. I went to help her up but realized that she wasn't laughing; she was crying. Her crying was soft at first but then became big, hot, gulping sobs. Shit. I walked over and put my hand on her shoulder. "Ma'am? Are you all right? Did that hillbilly steal your money?"

She stopped herself from crying and looked up at me for the first time. She did that thing that dogs do when they don't understand what you're saying. Where the dog will tilt its head to one side and look at you quizzically. That's when I noticed, through the tear-streaked eyeliner and the cheap, green-apple-scented lip gloss, just how much this lady looked like my good friend Jim Belushi!! It was uncanny! It was as if Jim himself had dressed up in a lady's dress and put makeup on. I sat staring at this odd lady, when she said, again in a deep voice, "What?!" She sounded like the Belush in that scene with the monkey robot from Mars in *Blues Brothers 2002*. I snapped out of it and helped her up.

"You look kinda like a friend of mine," I said. "Have you ever seen *Mr. Destiny*? It's about this asshole, and a magic bartender gives him a wish—"

"Hey, look, you dumb motherfucker, leave me the fuck alone," the lady interrupted. "I don't know if you noticed, but I'm not exactly having the greatest day."

"Oh, I'm sorry, it's just that—"

"Yeah, yeah, yeah." The lady then suddenly softened her look toward me. She seemed to be studying me the way an ape does when it wants a banana. "Jesus," she said tenderly, "you really don't get it, do you?" She brushed my one hair out of my eyes and touched my cheek. "You're sweet."

"Oh, well, thanks . . . uh . . ." It was starting to get even weirder. I got a sense that this lady wanted to thank me in a way that I wasn't very comfortable with. Then, in her thick Chicago-style accent, she said, "Do you want a date?"

"Oh, no, that's all right, I'm—"

"Come on. I'll suck your balls through your cock and then fuck 'em back on for forty bucks."

"Uh . . . huh?" I said, not sure that I heard her correctly. "Look, I gotta get going."

"Sure," she said, and dropped her hands to the ground. She hoisted herself up, wiped away her running mascara, and sniffed.

"Look at me. I'm a mess." She half laughed. "What the fuck happened to me? One minute you're giving a naïve intern at the House of Blues a hummer, and the next thing you know . . ." She trailed off and just stood there. She started to cry again, and that's when I took my cue.

I quietly got back in the car and headed out to Providence. I never got my snacks, but it was just as well. When I got to the end of the truck stop, I glanced at my rearview mirror, just in time to see the lady fix herself up and then slowly and sadly walk into the men's room and shut the door behind her. She made the same mistake twice! No wonder she's so miserable. Oh, well. I can't wait to tell my good buddy Jim Belushi about this one! He's gonna freak!!

See ya later kittens,
David

This is reprinted with permission from Playboy *magazine, whom I will never write for or patronize until the guy who hired me to do this piece is fired. This is the piece as I originally wrote it, but this fucking asshole goes and, without ever consulting me, adds his own lame jokes! Without ever mentioning it. That should be illegal, I believe. So now attached to my name is this piece with some of my stuff removed and his corny, obvious jokes added. Infuriating. I think the original is pretty good, so I'm including it in this book. Why not? It's called "Letter from the Future," and it was written a long, long time ago.*

Letter from the Future

HELLO, I AM FROM THE FUTURE. MY NAME IS TULLY SPETERTRENCH, and I am writing from my home state of Baja California Mexico California. The year is 2118. I would normally just use my Teleporter 3000™ and simply hand deliver the letter, but my teleporter got fucked up after the Not Enough Beer Riots of last quarter, so here it is. I have mailed it to a Mail Boxes, Etc. in the fall of '98, but we all know how lame the post office is, so who knows when it will get there. By the way, how much are stamps back then? Now they cost over two chickens apiece!

Anyhoo, hello there.

I woke up this morning to the official headline floating above my bed-like Pseudobed™. It read, "Nigger Elected President!" I couldn't believe it. A black man was in the White House. Jason Nigger had actually won. Mr. Nigger was able to overcome an unfortunate and ironic last name to claim the third most powerful position (more powerful are the positions of vice president and Emmy Award winner for Best Actress in a Dramatic Series) in the United States of America and Friends©. Personally, I had "rooted" (as voting is now called) for Devry Ahmad, a pre-post-op transsexual and scion of the wealthy Ahmad family. The Ahmads made their fortune in the artificial heart sauce business, creating over twenty different sauces for artificial hearts. I didn't mind Nigger, but I was swayed by Ahmad's promise of a free maid for every true American citizen. Oh, well. There are some things I'm looking forward to with this new administration. I've seen so many pictures of the olden days when there used to be snow on the artificial trees. If the energy policies are reversed, maybe I'll get to experience that without having to use the Teleporter™.

After I woke up and popped a few Shower Pills®™, I put one of my penises (evolution!) in the penis scanner and left my quadrent for workfun at the local Water®™ Treatment Plant. Officially my workfun title is Head of Crybabies. I guess I should explain, when the last source of fresh water was poisoned in the Year of the Officially Recognized Lord 2042, the country instituted a bold and exciting new plan to replenish our Water®™ supply. Desalinization of tears! So, after it became legal to clone immigrants, Senate Pro-Tem Wal-Mart (R-America) came upon the solution of torturing them and extracting their tears! Now Water®™ only costs fourteen tap dances! When I got to my workfun station, my boss, Angela Lansbury's Cousin the Third, told me that she needed to see me in her office. "Your orifice?" I asked, thereby fulfilling my pun quota of the day. "Very good," she replied, "but seriously, I need to see you in my office."

When I got to her office she motioned me over to her bed.

I took off my jacket, put on a hat, and crawled in. She told her assistdog to forward her calls to the bed. The assistdog barked her understanding and nudged the door shut behind us. I was nervous because I rarely let anybody see me in a hat, much less my boss, but here I was.

"You have a beautiful hat," she said rather coyly. "Do you mind if I fuck with it?" "No. No, of course not, Ms. Habigan. Go right ahead." She took off the hat, put it on her head, and then knocked it off with her tongue. I hadn't seen a trick like that since my great-great-great-grandfather took me to the Jim Rose Circus Circus Casino in Las Vegas. We had a couple of minutes of sex, and then she fired me. I had a feeling this was going to happen and had a contingency plan for earning money. I collected my severence pay, cashed out, went home, got in my Teleporter™, ported back to 1999, invested in American flags manufactured in China by prison labor (I also invested in Chinese prison labor), and then went back to my bank account. Voila! The old "Teleporter Switcheroo." I can't believe it took me that long to figure out an ending to this little story.

Thank you,
David Cross

An Afterthought

As this was going to press and I was skimming it over for one last time but not really paying that much attention because I had already gone over it before, my mind started drifting, and it occurred to me how much subject matter I left out. Or, didn't cover, might be a more appropriate thing to write, since I can always cover it later in a second book (if you'd be so generous enough to have me) and I didn't think of it to include initially, so it wasn't knowingly omitted. Anyway, I realized that I've written about the dangerous lunacy of the more prevalent and obvious religions, specifically the sexist, sadly insular, and antiquated demands of extreme Judaism, but have barely commented on the criminality and immoral depravity of Islam (which translates to, literally, "be in submission" to God). Nor of the attendant dangers of Sharia law to not just all women and unbearded men but most of humanity and its very future on this planet.

When this book was written, we didn't have a new president yet, let alone the first blackish president. We thought it might be a woman!! Or worse, an Oldie. Can you imagine!! Ewwwww! As a country and world, we were economically only sorta fucked, not super-insanely fucked as we are now. We were still in a seemingly predominately right-leaning country who proudly yelled their love of Jesus and of watching minor celebrities competitively dance against each other while mindlessly parroting the cherry-picked half facts that supported our ideas of whether global warming was a real, urgent issue or a scam. Or whether members of the Democratic Congress were not so secretly American-hating communists who wanted nothing more than to cede America to a figment of those on the right's imagination. Or whether the Republicans secretly want to facilitate Armageddon in order to show everyone else that they were right the whole time and snicker and "tssk" as they ascend to eat grapes fed to them by the most attractive American angels imaginable in a temperature-controlled Heaven with questionable gravity issues.

There's so much more to write about! There is not one mention of liposuction, for instance—the lazy man's (mostly woman's, though) way to a slimmer, trimmer, unhealthy you. Certainly not enough about "Life Coaches," perhaps the single greatest example of our crybaby culture that clearly has too much money and is all too happy to play the victim.

And in order not be overly negative, I didn't really touch upon some of the things that make America great, like our propaganda machine, the best in history. And how we are the single greatest culture that forcibly exports that culture and ideas for how to best live your life to the rest of the world (who gladly lap it up) in history! Oh well. If I do get a chance to put together a second book (hey, people always have to shit, right?), I will include these subjects and many, many more.

Oh, and one last thing; Gil Scott-Heron once famously wrote that "the revolution will not be televised." I'm not so sure about that. But I do know that it will be Twittered. And that's *real* progress.

Acknowledgments

WRITING A BOOK IS NOT EASY, UNLESS IT'S JUST A COLLECTION OF your shitty stand-up routines that you don't do anymore, with full-size childish illustrations on every other page. Then yes, it's easy. But that's not this book. This book was thoroughly and intensively researched. It was vetted by Colonel Harman DeWitt and given its final "thumbs up" by the editorial staff at *The National Review*. But it wasn't just me who wrote this book. I mean, yes it was just me literally but figuratively there were so many additional authors. So with them in mind I would like to thank the following, without whom, through their selflessness and friendship, this book would or would not have happened:

Suzanne Estherburg at Connecticut Muffins for her delicious Patriotberry Muffins. They kept me going through a tough summer.

My agent, whom I've never met and who, just for making a couple of phone calls, receives 10 percent of all pretaxed income from this book.

Tammy, Brenda, Ng, Cee-Cee, Gordon, Miz Tuffstuff, Big Lips, The Butcher, Creamzie, Puddin Pops, Misty, Pearl Neck,

Tonya, Heather, Lil' Tits, Scrim Shaw, Cum Eyes, Turtle, Poochy, Princess, Tiny Cock Grinder, and Necromancer at Grand Central Publishing. You folks were my patient guides through this whole ordeal. Each one of you contributed to making it slightly less horrific. You reached inside of yourselves and saw how to make a book not only smile but gurgle a bit and then spit up on your shoulder. Thank you.

The boys down at Q107.5, playing the greatest collection of soft hits from the '70s, '80s, '90s, and now. Keep the Al Stewart coming, y'all!

Ethan Allen, your sensible turn-of-the-century furniture helped this old man get comfortable and get to sleep at a respectable hour.

Dev and Shonalli Paktika at 4th Street Samosa's 'n' Things.

The gang down at Rock Honda off Route 17.

The Gertrude Stein Institute for the lovely gift of the hand-carved birthing tub.

Everyone who priff-read this.

Buttercup Henderson for his stoicism. You are the wings of a bird flying high above a verdant valley of dreams and well wishes. This is true, by the way.

The good folks at the Dallas/Ft. Worth Airport TSA, you are all heroes. How you manage the strength and fortitude to do what you do is beyond me and an inspiration for us all. Keep fighting the good fight!

The great Harland McYannish, cantor to the stars. Hey bro'! Save some of that charoset for me!!!

All the middle relievers for the Washington Nationals, except for Saul Rivera.

Celine and Dave at Monsanto.

Jomo Grafficha, Burr Hispy, Jordy Zapp, Gush Tushy, Mal Christ, Yunel Winfart, Flick Dristan, Pooey Puff, and everyone at the Funny Name Institute.

Trevor Cleveland, my Shaq-Fu teacher.

The Ho-Chunk nation for keeping the loosest slots in the Midwest. Over 99 percent payouts!

Vandana Hanfannan. Your stories of courage and daring at the DMV filled me with shame and moisture. I will never forget you, lady.

Grilleth Bear. You came and you stopped me from shaking. And I need you today.

Toliver, Sissy, Bleedle, and Ponch Ahoy. Fuck it, let's make it the whole Ahoy family! You guys really took me under your wingdings and things.

And lastly, thanks to *Battlestar Galactica*.